Definition of SERIOUS AND COMPLEX MEDICAL CONDITIONS

Carole A. Chrvala, Ph.D., and Steven Sharfstein, M.D., *Editors*

Committee on Serious and Complex Medical Conditions

Division of Health Care Services

INSTITUTE OF MEDICINE

NATIONAL ACADEMY PRESS
Washington, DC

NATIONAL ACADEMY PRESS • 2101 Constitution Avenue, N.W. • Washington, D.C. 20418

NOTICE: The project that is the subject of this report was approved by the Governing Board of the National Research Council, whose members are drawn from the councils of the National Academy of Sciences, the National Academy of Engineering, and the Institute of Medicine. The members of the committee responsible for the report were chosen for their special competences and with regard for appropriate balance.

The Institute of Medicine was chartered in 1970 by the National Academy of Sciences to enlist distinguished members of the appropriate professions in the examination of policy matters pertaining to the health of the public. In this, the Institute acts both under the Academy's 1863 congressional charter responsibility to be an adviser to the federal government and its own initiative in identifying issues of medical care, research, and education. Dr. Kenneth I. Shine is president of the Institute of Medicine.

Support for this study was provided by the Department of Health and Human Services, Health Care Financing Administration, Contract No. 500-99-0002. The views presented are those of the Institute of Medicine Committee on Serious and Complex Medical Conditions and are not necessarily those of the funding organization.

International Standard Book No. 0-309-06640-9

Additional copies of this report are available for sale from:

National Academy Press
2101 Constitution Avenue, N.W.
Box 285
Washington, DC 20055

Call (800) 624-6242 or (202) 334-3313 (in the Washington metropolitan area), or visit the NAP's on-line bookstore at **www.nap.edu.**

For more information about the Institute of Medicine, visit the IOM home page at **www.iom.edu.**

Copyright 1999 by the National Academy of Sciences. All rights reserved.

Printed in the United States of America

The serpent has been a symbol of long life, healing, and knowledge among almost all cultures and religions since the beginning of recorded history. The image adopted as a logotype by the Institute of Medicine is based on a relief carving from ancient Greece, now held by the Staatliche Museen in Berlin.

COMMITTEE ON SERIOUS AND COMPLEX MEDICAL CONDITIONS

STEVEN SHARFSTEIN, M.D. (*Chair*), Sheppard Pratt Health Systems, Baltimore, Maryland
WILLIAM GOLDEN, M.D., University of Arkansas for Medical Sciences, Little Rock
SAM HO, M.D., Pacificare Health Systems, Santa Ana, California
SHARON LEVINE, M.D., The Permanente Medical Group, Oakland, California
KATHLEEN McGINLEY, Ph.D., The Arc of the United States, Governmental Affairs Office, Washington, D.C.
GARTH SPLINTER, M.D., M.B.A., University of Oklahoma College of Medicine, Chief Medical Officer, University Hospitals Trust, and Former CEO of the Oklahoma Health Care Authority, Oklahoma City
NANCY WHITELAW, Ph.D., Henry Ford Health System, Detroit, Michigan

Staff
CAROLE A. CHRVALA, Study Director
JANET CORRIGAN, Director, Division of Health Care Services
DONNA DUNCAN, Administrative Assistant, Division of Health Promotion and Disease Prevention
KELLY PIKE, Project Assistant
KELLY NORSINGLE, Project Assistant

Acknowledgments

Preparation of this report would not have been possible without the guidance and expertise of numerous individuals. Although it is not possible to mention by name all of those who contributed to its work, the committee wants to express its gratitude to a number of groups and individuals for their special contributions.

Special thanks are extended to Judith Bragdon, Center for Health Plans and Providers, Health Care Financing Administration; Patricia Kurtz, Center for Medicaid and State Operations, Health Care Financing Administration; and Gavin Kennedy, Office of the Assistant Secretary for Planning and Evaluation, Department of Health and Human Services, for the guidance they provided to clarify the charge to the committee and facilitate identification of the major issues to be considered as the committee undertook its charge. The committee is especially appreciative of the efforts of Tony Hausner, Ph.D., of the Health Care Financing Administration, for serving as the project officer and providing information relevant to the committee's deliberations.

Sincere thanks go to all of the participants at the workshop convened on June 14, 1999. The speakers (Appendix B) gave generously of their time and expertise to help inform and guide the committee's work. We are particularly appreciative of the efforts of David Nerenz, Ph.D., director, Center for Health Services Research, Henry Ford Health System. His commissioned paper on "Definitions of Serious and Complex Medical Conditions: Alternatives and Implications" was seriously considered in the deliberations of the committee and his advice throughout the committee's work has been greatly appreciated. We also recognize the careful and thoughtful efforts of Florence Poillen to edit the text of this report.

The committee extends special thanks to the dedicated and hardworking staff at the Institute of Medicine. The expertise and leadership of Janet Corrigan, director of the Division of Health Care Services, Institute of Medicine, helped to ensure that this report met the highest standards of quality. Study Director Carole A. Chrvala's expertise in study management and organization, as well as her commitment to the topic of defining serious or complex medical conditions, successfully advanced the progress of the committee's report through several drafts and a rapid report review process. Kelly Norsingle served as project assistant and worked closely with the study director on many aspects of this study. She coordinated the logistics for all committee meetings and conference calls as well as completing all of the arrangements for the workshop. Kelly Pike and Donna Duncan contributed their skills and knowledge in preparing this report for its publication.

Other Institute of Medicine staff provided valuable guidance in the areas of both substance and process including the Administrative Office, Office of Contracts and Grants, Office of Finance, and the Report Review Committee. Kathleen Stratton, Lyla Hernandez, and Catharyn Liverman provided invaluable technical and moral support to the study director that helped her to carry this project to successful completion.

Individuals chosen for their diverse perspectives and expertise in health services research, health care insurance and economic policies, clinical issues, and delivery of services by health care plans reviewed this report in draft form. This review was conducted in accordance with procedures approved by the National Research Council's Report Review Committee. The purpose of this independent review is to provide candid and critical comments that will assist the IOM in making the published report as sound as possible and to ensure that the report meets institutional standards for objectivity, evidence, and responsiveness to the study charge. The review comments and draft manuscript remain confidential to protect the integrity of the deliberative process. We wish to thank the following individuals for their participation in the review of this report: Christine K. Cassel, M.D., Mount Sinai Hospital School of Medicine; Kristine M. Gebbie, R.N., Dr.P.H., Columbia University; Lynn Gerber, M.D., National Institutes of Health, Clinical Center; Stanley Jones, Consultant, Sheperdstown, WV; Judith Krauss, M.S.N., F.A.A.N.; Lee N. Newcomer, M.D., United Health Group; Peter Rabins, M.D., Johns Hopkins University Hospital; Deborah Spitalnik, Ph.D., Robert Wood Johnson Medical School; Barbara Vickrey, M.D., M.P.H., University of California Los Angeles, Department of Neurology; Edward Wagner, M.D., Group Health Cooperative of Puget Sound; and Sandra Harmon-Weiss, Aetna US Healthcare. Although these individuals provided many constructive comments and suggestions, responsibility for the final content of this report rests solely with the authoring committee and the Institute of Medicine.

Finally, the committee would like to thank the chair, Steven S. Sharfstein, M.D., for his outstanding work, leadership, and dedication to this project.

Contents

EXECUTIVE SUMMARY   1

1 INTRODUCTION   15
Charge to the Institute of Medicine, 15
Scope and Organization of This Report, 17
Definitions of Serious and Complex Medical Conditions: Alternatives
    and Implications, 18

**2 CHALLENGES IN HEALTH CARE DELIVERY FOR PATIENTS
WITH SERIOUS AND COMPLEX MEDICAL CONDITIONS**   34
Quality of Health Care, 35
Access to Care, 38
Health Care Cost Containment, 40

3 CONCLUSIONS AND RECOMMENDATIONS   45
Introduction, 43
Conclusions, 54

REFERENCES   55

APPENDIXES
A   Workshop to Define Serious or Complex Medical Conditions, 65
B   Speakers Biographies, 107
C   Workshop Agenda, 110
D   Workshop Participants, 112
E   Committee Biographies, 113

Definition of
SERIOUS AND COMPLEX MEDICAL CONDITIONS

Executive Summary

In response to a request by the Health Care Financing Administration (HCFA), the Institute of Medicine proposed a study to examine definitions of serious or complex medical conditions and related issues. Health plans participating in the Medicare+Choice program are required to have procedures approved by HCFA for (1) identification of individuals (enrollees) with serious or complex medical conditions; (2) assessment of these conditions, including medical procedures to diagnose and monitor them on an ongoing basis; and (3) establishment and implementation of a treatment plan appropriate to these conditions, with an adequate number of direct access visits to specialists to accommodate the treatment plan. Such treatment plans must be time-specific and updated periodically by the primary care physician.

The charge to the Institute of Medicine requested that a committee be established to respond to the following questions:

1. Should health plans be required to have a general policy for dealing with serious or complex medical conditions, or should HCFA provide more specific guidance as to the types of beneficiaries to be included in this requirement?

2. If specific guidance is to be provided by HCFA, what are the advantages and disadvantages of alternative measurement approaches (e.g., activities of daily living scales, listing of medical conditions)? How feasible would it be for plans to implement such guidance about specific measurement approaches? Should the need for coordination with community and social service agencies be included in the definition of "complex conditions"?

3. What are the implications of alternative definitions for Medicaid and commercial programs, when applied to Medicare beneficiaries who are dual eligible?

A seven-member committee was appointed to address these issues. Throughout the course of this study, the committee has been aware of the fact that the topic addressed by this report concerns one of the most critical issues confronting HCFA, health care plans and providers, and patients today. The Medicare+Choice regulations focus on the most vulnerable populations in need of medical care and other services—those with serious or complex medical conditions. Caring for these highly vulnerable populations poses a number of challenges. The committee believes, however, that the current state of clinical and research literature does not adequately address all of the challenges and issues relevant to the identification and care of these patients.

As the committee accepted its charge, it followed general principles of scientific investigation, including reliance on evidence-based research to support its findings, conclusions, and recommendations. Several key activities formed the basis of the committee's final conclusions and recommendations to HCFA. The committee conducted a comprehensive review of pertinent literature and research and convened a workshop on June 14, 1999. (See Appendix A for a summary of the workshop proceedings.) The purpose of this workshop was to elicit the knowledge, expertise, and opinions of professionals with involvement in issues associated with the identification and treatment of persons with serious or complex medical conditions.

Topics addressed by the literature review and the workshop included the following: (1) proposed definitions of serious or complex medical conditions; (2) methods to screen at-risk populations; (3) development and implementation of care plans; (4) strategies to ensure continuity, quality, access, and coordination of care; and (5) issues of payment for the service needs of patients with serious or complex medical conditions. Findings from the literature review and the workshop were supplemented by a commissioned paper (see Chapter 1) that analyzed objectives to be met by the development of definitions for serious or complex medical conditions and also outlined the strengths and weaknesses of alternative definitions.

As the committee began its deliberations about the charge and considered information from the literature review, workshop, and commissioned paper, it recognized a need to identify a patient population that would have diverse and complicated needs requiring a multidisciplinary, comprehensive care management approach to ensure the best possible medical, social, and mental health outcomes. The committee acknowledges that the potential universe of patients with such serious or complex medical conditions is likely to be very large. Rather than developing recommendations to immediately address this large population, the committee proposes a description of a smaller and more confined patient population to include those patients with serious AND complex conditions. The committee describes a serious and complex condition as one that is persistent, substantially disabling or life threatening, and that requires treatments and interventions across a broad scope of medical, social, and mental health services. The committee contends that patients with serious AND complex conditions are those with the greatest need for the specialized services of a multidisciplinary group of professionals whose services can be coordinated through a broad care management approach.

Relying on a description that is limited in scope to serious AND complex conditions is intended to allow health care plans to develop the skills and resources necessary to conduct case finding among their enrollees for such conditions. In addition, the committee believes that health plans will develop the resources and skills essential to the provision of broad strategies of care management. As expertise is established in both case finding and care management for these patients and as resources are identified to support broad care management strategies for a larger number of beneficiaries, the description of eligible populations can be expanded to include those with serious but not complex conditions as well as those with complex but not serious conditions.

The committee believes that access to medical specialists is only one potential element of the broad strategies of care management these patients require. The committee does not feel that the narrow focus on "access to specialists" appropriately addresses the complexity of needs for patients with serious and complex medical conditions. In fact, it is the opinion of this committee that patients with serious and complex medical conditions may be at higher risk from inadequate coordination of proactive care across a broad spectrum of service needs than merely from lack of access to medical specialists.

Rather, such patient populations will benefit from access to multidisciplinary, specialized services that may or may not include direct access to medical specialists. Such specialized services may include, but not be limited to, inpatient and outpatient medical care; physical, occupational, and speech therapy; behavioral and mental health care; home care services; nutritional support; transportation services; rehabilitation training; and long-term care in skilled nursing facilities, nursing homes, or hospices. Delivery of these services may require the involvement of primary care physicians; medical and surgical specialists; nurses and nurse specialists; social workers; occupational, speech, and physical therapists; behavioral and mental health professionals; rehabilitation specialists; community-based service providers; and allied health professionals such as lay health workers. Services provided by these specialists should be proactive when possible to avoid further complications and exacerbation of disease and disability.

The committee also directed its attention to issues relevant to the specific elements of treatment plans for beneficiaries considered to have a serious and complex medical condition. Of particular concern is the identification of strategies of care management that will likely result in the highest level of functional status and quality of life. The success of this care management strategy will depend on the collaborative efforts of a multidisciplinary team of professionals as indicated above to address the full spectrum of physical, social, and mental health needs of patients with serious and complex conditions. In addition, the committee considered issues concerning monitoring and evaluation of efforts to identify patients with serious or complex conditions; the development and implementation of treatment plans; and the modification of such plans to accommodate changes in patients' physical, social, and mental health status. The following conclusions and recommendations are based on consideration of these diverse issues.

Recommendation 1: The establishment of an administrative definition for serious and complex medical conditions by the Health Care Financing Administration would be premature at this time.

It is the opinion of this committee that the state of current clinical and research literature does not support development of an operational definition for serious and complex medical conditions. While there are a large number of potential ways to conduct case finding to identify patients with serious and complex medical conditions, many of these have significant limitations. For example, disease classification systems such as the diagnosis-related groups, diagnostic cost groups, and the *International Classification of Diseases—Ninth Edition* lack the sensitivity and specificity required to effectively distinguish between patients with acute care needs and those who need more extensive treatment and service arrays. The validity of patient classification efforts (e.g., diagnosis-related groups) and functional status classification systems (e.g., the Karnofsky and SF-36 scales) has not yet been established. Efforts to develop case-mix-adjusted reimbursement systems to ensure cost-effectiveness and high-quality interventions for patients with serious and complex conditions are still in the early stages or are limited to only a single disease category. Similarly, efforts to develop standardized protocols for care coordination, continuity of care, care management strategies, and service reimbursement plans have met with varying degrees of success.

Clinical research relevant to defining patient populations with serious and complex conditions and developing the most effective care protocols to respond to patient needs is evolving rapidly, but only preliminary results are available. For example, research in correlating patient volume with patient outcomes, differentiating access to services as a function of health plan benefits, and addressing variations in quality of care has just begun to yield meaningful results about particular groups of patients. The committee anticipates that this research will continue to evolve and will provide more definitive conclusions to guide the efforts of health plans to identify patients with serious and complex medical conditions and ensure appropriate levels of treatment and care management. As the science base is strengthened, so too will be the ability of HCFA and health plans to correctly identify patients with serious and complex medical conditions who would benefit from broad strategies of care management.

Recognizing these limitations, the committee recommends that plans first focus their attentions on patient populations with conditions that are serious AND complex. These conditions are described as persistent, substantially disabling or life threatening, and requiring treatments and interventions across a broad scope of medical, social, and mental health services. Plans will require time to develop expertise and resources to develop methods of case finding and provision of an integrated care management approach for these patients. As such expertise is developed and resources are allocated, plans can then expand their efforts to include patients with serious but not complex conditions and those with complex but not serious conditions.

> **Recommendation 2:** The committee recommends that the Health Care Financing Administration should provide *guidance* to health plans to assist their efforts to identify patients with serious and complex medical conditions. Specifically, the committee recommends the following language be used to facilitate efforts of plans to identify their enrollees with "serious and complex conditions": "A *serious and complex* condition is one that is persistent and substantially disabling or life threatening that requires treatments and services across a variety of domains of care to ensure the best possible outcomes for each unique patient or member."

The committee recognizes the importance at this time of providing health plans with **guidance** to facilitate operationalization of their own definitions of serious and complex medical conditions. This guidance includes a description of a serious and complex medical condition as one that is persistent and substantially disabling or life threatening that requires treatments and services across a variety of domains of care. The committee reviewed a number of possible categories of conditions that might be considered serious and complex. These are discussed in Chapter 1 of this report and include, but are not limited to, life threatening conditions, conditions that cause serious disability without necessarily being life threatening, conditions associated with severe consequences, conditions affecting multiple organ systems, conditions requiring coordination of management by multiple specialties, and conditions requiring treatments that carry a risk of serious complications.

As noted above, clinical research to identify patient populations with serious and complex medical conditions and develop the most effective care management strategies to respond to patient needs is evolving rapidly, with only preliminary results available. The committee believes, however, that the current state of clinical and research literature does not adequately address all of the challenges and issues relevant to the identification and care of these patients. These issues include, but are not limited to, identification of methods and criteria that can be applied to screen enrollees for the presence of serious and complex conditions; development of strategies for proper care and management of the complex array of medical, social, and mental health problems confronting these patients; development of strategies to evaluate the effectiveness, efficacy, and efficiency of different strategies of care management; and ongoing research to ensure continuous improvements in the care of these patients. Health care service research is only beginning to emerge with initial findings relevant to these issues.

The committee anticipates that this research will continue to evolve and provide more definitive conclusions to guide the efforts of health plans to identify patients with serious and complex medical conditions and help plans to provide appropriate levels of treatment and care management. The committee urges health care plans, in collaboration with federal agencies and research institutions, to support this ongoing research and facilitate a synthesis of emerging results. As the science base is strengthened, so too will be the ability of HCFA and health plans to correctly identify patients with serious and complex medical conditions who would benefit from a broad care management strategy, including those with serious but not complex or complex but not serious conditions.

Recommendation 3: The committee recommends that health care plans develop a broad strategy for care management to enable patients and providers to achieve the best possible outcomes for each unique patient or member with a serious and complex medical condition.

This care management strategy should include, but not necessarily be limited to, case finding; screening and selection; problem assessment and identification of strengths; development of treatment or care plans; implementation of care plans with an emphasis on proactive interventions; and monitoring of care plan implementation and outcomes.

The treatments for individuals with serious and complex medical conditions will inevitably vary due to many factors, including characteristics of the individual patient and the patient's social situation, characteristics of individual providers, provider organizations, health care plans, resources in the community, health plan benefits, and so forth. Although these factors will vary for all patients, they have less impact on preventive care (e.g., immunizations) and acute care (e.g., setting a broken arm) interventions. Successful outcomes for persons with serious and complex medical conditions will rest upon a diverse mix of medical, social, functional, financial, and psychological factors, as well as on how these factors mesh with a community's health and social services resources. There is no single guideline that can prescribe the care or treatments for persons with serious and complex medical conditions.

The committee's recommendations concerning elements of the care management strategy have been derived, in part, from existing publications (Case Management Society of America, 1996; HMO Workgroup on Care Management, 1999). A brief explanation for each of the recommended steps in the care process is provided below.

Case finding refers to methods for identifying persons who may have a serious and complex medical condition. Utilization of the committee's recommended description for serious and complex conditions can facilitate efforts by health plans and providers to identify possible categories of patients for whom case finding should be conducted. Depending on the organization of a health plan and its provider group(s), case finding methods may include electronic searching of administrative databases; phone screening of new or existing members; referral by patient or family member; referral by a clinician or other professional; or notification by an emergency room, hospital, nursing home, or other provider organization.

Case screening and selection outline a process for deciding exactly which patients meet a plan's criteria for serious and complex medical conditions. These criteria should be established by each health plan with review by HCFA. Examples of selection criteria might include factors such as diagnostic codes, patient age, presence of comorbidities, severity of illness or disability, duration of a disability, and so forth. It is expected that patients meeting these criteria would benefit from coordinated care management.

The next step in the care process should involve an assessment of the patient's problems and strengths. This is a tool for gathering information about the patient's medical, social, functional, and financial status that will be used to further determine his or her need for care management and the resources available to access the necessary services.

Treatment or care planning is also recommended by the committee as an essential element of a care management strategy for patients with serious and complex medical conditions. Such planning supports the development of individualized, goal-focused care plans (based on assessment findings and drawing on evidence-based treatments when available) to provide a guide for delineating patient, provider, and plan responsibilities for accessing and coordinating needed services.

The care management strategy also demands that steps be taken to ensure the implementation of care plans. Execution of the care management plan includes strategies and tactics for providing or purchasing needed services, or for linking patients to covered services, services available in the community, or those for which the patient will have to pay. It also includes advocating for the provision of informal services by family, friends, and neighbors.

The final step of the care process is monitoring implementation and outcomes of the care management strategy. This can be based upon periodic reviews of a patient's status and treatments to determine whether goals are being achieved, whether interventions and treatments continue to be appropriate, whether there is a medical need for continued services, or whether proactive care is required to address potential or emerging new problems. This type of monitoring can also include measurements to assess the impact of care management and treatment on clinical, functional, cost, and satisfaction outcomes.

Throughout the entire care management strategy for persons with serious and complex medical conditions, three principles should be evident. First, the care management strategy should reflect a commitment to continuity and coordination of care, as described among the requirements for National Committee for Quality Assurance accreditation. This entails monitoring continuity and coordination activities, analyzing data to identify opportunities for improvement, and taking actions to bring about improvements, as indicated. Second, the care process should include multidisciplinary perspectives and treatments, as appropriate. The care of persons with serious and complex medical conditions may require the assessment and treatment expertise of primary care providers; medical and surgical specialists; nurses and nurse specialists; social workers; pharmacists; occupational, speech, and physical therapists; rehabilitation specialists; behavioral and mental health professionals; and community-based services providers and resources. Access to expertise from these various disciplines should be available as needed. Third, and perhaps most important, patients and their family members should be involved at every step so that the care process incorporates the patient's expectations and preferences and documents the patient's role in achieving treatment goals.

The committee's recommendations concerning the care management process for patients with serious and complex conditions assumes patient willingness to collaborate with a multidisciplinary team of providers in the development and implementation of that plan. In those instances where a patient or family member declines such participation, appropriate documentation should be entered into the patient record. The presence of such documentation should be considered by HCFA as evidence that a good faith effort has been made by the plan to involve the patient and family in the development of the case management plan.

Recommendation 4: The committee recommends that health plans design and implement strategies for routine screening and selection to identify those beneficiaries with serious and complex medical conditions. These strategies should be consistent with the guidance outlined in Recommendation 2 to determine which patients meet a plan's threshold for serious and complex medical conditions and would benefit from a coordinated care management strategy.

The committee recommends that health plans identify specific categories of patients or health conditions for which screening for the presence of serious and complex conditions should occur on a routine basis. Examples of such categories are provided in Chapter 1. The committee is of the opinion that screening a health care plan's entire population of enrollees is not a feasible, cost-effective, or efficient method of identifying subpopulations with serious and complex medical conditions. The committee feels strongly, however, that early efforts to develop screening methodologies should not be prescriptive; rather, innovation should be encouraged. Documentation of locally derived methods by plans will result in extensive nationwide experience that can be assessed and can lead to the identification of best practices and subsequent standardized methods for ongoing routine screening of patient populations.

The appropriate application of resources by a health plan to patients with serious and complex medical conditions requires the identification of those individuals whose health outcomes would benefit by such designation. For the purposes of this report, the committee has not included patients suffering from acute conditions that might require coordinated delivery of sophisticated medical services to treat complications of acute decompensation. On the other hand, many patients who have endured prolonged hospitalization for an acute medical condition may subsequently need coordinated long-term care to maximize their rehabilitation potential; to treat persistent sequelae of the disease processes that resulted from the acute, severe illness; and to ensure that they receive proactive care to prevent further exacerbation of the illness or disability.

Conceptually, various methodologies could be applied to administrative databases that could produce relevant lists of patients with serious and complex medical conditions who would be likely to benefit from written care management plans. High-cost patients, for example, might merit designation as having serious and complex conditions. Some of these individuals, however, may have undergone a single event such as bypass surgery that is self-limited and not appropriate for such designation. In contrast, others will have conditions, such as organ transplants, disabling traumatic injury, and HIV/AIDS, that clearly require ongoing medical attention and resources to sustain or improve their health status. Aside from costs, certain diagnostic entities could be identified for designation as serious and complex medical conditions. Examples of such entities could include progressive, degenerative disorders, active collagen vascular disease, and metastatic cancers. The committee does not believe it is feasible at this time to create an all-encompassing list of diagnoses appropriate for designation as serious and complex conditions. Indeed, within any diagnostic label, there exists a continuum of disease and disability that requires varying degrees of medical and other health-related supports.

Beneficiary survey tools could supplement the use of administrative data sets to identify appropriate patients. Questionnaires that quantify functional status could assist plans in capturing individuals who need special attention in the outpatient setting to improve or sustain functional capacity or physiological stability. Similarly, home health agencies or medical professionals could identify frail elderly patients who require care management to sustain homeostasis. These agents could refer patients' names to health plans for development of a formal management program for serious and complex medical conditions. Such patients could include those of advanced age (over 85) with several comorbid medical conditions such as congestive heart failure, chronic renal failure, and diabetes. These persistent conditions in concert with reduced cognitive functioning or physical capacity to sustain daily living activities produce a constellation of physiological deficits that require supportive health care services for the patient to maintain independent living in a community setting.

There are several reasons why it is essential to the care of persons with serious and complex medical conditions that screening and selection of a plan's designated patient categories or conditions occurs on a routine basis. First, periodic screening allows the multidisciplinary care team to adjust the care management approach as patient needs change over time. Second, routine screening is essential to identify new patients with serious and complex medical conditions. Third, it ensures that persons who are no longer considered to have a serious or complex condition will be identified and services adjusted accordingly, which could result in cost benefits.

The committee believes that over time, the health care system will identify reliable, accurate screening techniques for populations of patients with serious and complex medical conditions. In many cases, timely identification will permit proactive, appropriate treatment at the level of the primary care provider. Nevertheless, even with robust methodologies in place, there will be patients and families who believe that they require additional resources or attention to adequately manage a persistent health condition. In instances in which a treatment plan is not mutually agreed upon, individuals should be able to appeal to the medical director of the provider group or health plan. The review process should be timely and should allow for both internal and independent external review.

Recommendation 5: The committee recommends that health care plans develop a care management strategy that integrates the participation of all those involved in the care of the patient, including primary care physicians; medical and surgical specialists; nurses and nurse specialists; behavioral and mental health specialists; physical, occupational, and speech therapists; social workers; allied health professionals; and community-based service providers.

The development of a collaborative care management strategy involving all those who participate in providing care to the individual patient is critical to the provision of care to patients with serious and complex conditions. The treatment plan serves several important functions within the care management strategy. First, it provides a road map and a guide to indicate direction of and demarcate landmarks in care management, making it easier to ensure that all providers involved in the patient's care share the same goals, and that these goals are accessible to the patient and the patient's family. Second, it provides a way to measure progress and the achievement of care goals, and it serves as a powerful communication and coordination tool among the participants involved in the care of the patient, avoiding overlapping or redundant efforts as well as gaps and inattention to components of care assumed to be the responsibility of others on the care team. Third, a treatment plan offers an opportunity to delineate which provider is taking responsibility for specific aspects of care.

Although there is currently no evidence to support the identification of a single format or model as superior to all others, the committee feels confident in recommending certain key components that should be part of any treatment plan for patients with serious and complex medical conditions. Specifically, the plan should involve the collaborative participation of all those taking part in the care of the patient, including primary care physicians; medical and surgical specialists; nurses and nurse specialists; physical, occupational, and speech therapists; rehabilitation specialists; behavioral and mental health specialists; social workers; allied health professionals; and community-based service providers.

The perspectives, health beliefs, and values of the patient and the patient's family should be taken into consideration, and the care management plan should be constructed in a culturally appropriate manner. Elements of the care management plan should be appropriate both for the age or life phase of each patient as well as the stage or severity of the health condition. This will ensure selection of treatment options that are responsive to the unique needs of patients of different age groups and with conditions of varying severity. The patient should be involved in the development of the plan and should have access to the plan.

The plan should be linked to relevant clinical practice guidelines and should reflect the process of adapting population-based clinical practice guidelines to the unique care and service needs of the individual. The treatment plan should cross areas of expertise and should address the need for coordination of care across the continuum of care delivery settings. The plan should be longitudinal, with accommodations for proactive interventions to prevent potential problems from arising, and it should also enable longitudinal assessment of outcomes. The treatment plan should be a living document that is periodically reviewed, updated, and tested for continuing relevance to the patient's circumstances (e.g., life phase) and clinical condition (e.g., disease stage).

Recommendation 6: The committee recommends that health care plans have programs in place to monitor care management plans for both process and outcomes for patients with serious and complex conditions at the level of population, patient, provider, and best practices of care.

The Health Care Financing Administration should establish a formal mechanism to evaluate a Medicare+Choice provider organization's program to monitor the outcomes of care for patients with serious and complex medical conditions. The committee recognizes that monitoring and evaluation programs will vary between health care plans but recommends that all programs include population-based monitoring of the outcomes of care for patients with serious and complex conditions, as well as individual case monitoring, assessment of provider interventions, and evaluation of best practices of care.

Assessment of population-based measures may include, but not be limited to, review of plan-wide policies and procedures; application of working definitions of serious and complex conditions; adoption of evidence-based clinical guidelines; review of health outcomes survey, patient satisfaction, and complaint data; and review of clinical outcomes data for patients with serious and complex medical conditions. Individual case monitoring may include, but not be limited to, analysis of complaint data, patient satisfaction, internal and external appeals of the care plan, and overturned denials. Evaluation and monitoring at the level of providers will include efforts to assess clinical quality of care, timeliness of care, and effectiveness of specific interventions. Best practices of care will be identified by data that describe clinical, functional, and patient satisfaction outcomes.

Recommendation 7: The committee recommends that the Health Care Financing Administration collaborate with federal, private,

and voluntary agencies, organizations, and consumers to establish an ongoing process to address policy issues to ensure continuous improvements in the care of populations with serious and complex medical conditions.

Access to providers with the appropriate training and expertise is important, but other issues must be addressed to ensure that beneficiaries with serious and complex conditions achieve the best possible outcomes. The committee recognizes that a number of these issues supersede activities that can be accomplished at the level of individual health plans. Issues that must be addressed include, but are not limited to, the following:

- *Payment.* The current Medicare capitated payment mechanisms for health plans are not risk adjusted and are derived from experience in the fee-for-service sector. These payment mechanisms may not provide adequate compensation to some health plans. Furthermore, health plans use a variety of methods to compensate individual providers and hospitals. Greater attention should be focused on the improved alignment of financial incentives at all levels to ensure appropriate payment for serious and complex cases through adequate funding and risk-adjusted payment systems.
- *Benefits.* Improving the care of persons with serious and complex medical conditions can be supported by ensuring that Medicare beneficiaries can choose among different health plans. When beneficiaries have multiple affordable options, they can select based upon their own evaluations of quality. Where benefits are provided through multiple payment programs (i.e., Medicare and Medicaid dual eligibles), coordination of benefit packages and eligibility requirements is critical. The movement of patients with serious and complex conditions into managed care holds the promise of greater health for these patients and therefore reduced expenditures for Medicaid programs due to reduced nursing home use. Prescription coverage for these patients would result in a direct reduction in state Medicaid prescription coverage expenses. Medicare requirements for management of patients with serious and complex conditions may also serve as the future basis for Medicaid managed care contracts.
- *Medicaid and Medicare Fee-for-Service Programs.* The committee was unable to address the third point of its charge with any degree of thoroughness. This is primarily due to the fact that the committee lacked sufficient information and time to conduct informed deliberations about the implications of alternative definitions for serious and complex medical conditions for Medicaid and commercial programs, especially when applied to Medicare beneficiaries who are dual eligible. The committee strongly recommends that HCFA, in collaboration with Medicare and Medicaid provider plans, establish this as a research priority. Resources and expertise should be allocated to conduct a study to define the relevant issues and generate possible approaches to address this question.

In the meantime, the committee suggests that the basic guidance provided in this report concerning the description of serious and complex medical conditions and recommendations concerning strategies for care management for this patient population should be extended to include Medicaid beneficiaries and those that are dual eligible. In addition, this guidance should apply to patients enrolled in fee-for-service Medicare programs. This should be a priority area for collaborative research on policy issues to ensure continuous improvements in the care of populations with serious and complex medical conditions covered by Medicaid and fee-for-service Medicare plans.

- *Consumer Education and Participation.* Many patients, especially those with persistent and disabling conditions, are ready and able to become more active participants in the care delivery process. Attempts should be made to increase patient participation in clinical decision-making and caregiving processes consistent with improving clinical outcomes and satisfaction.

- *Professional Training.* To serve persons with serious and complex medical conditions, an aggressive strategy must be developed to educate and train health professionals to provide appropriate care for this population. There is currently a great undersupply of persons trained in care management processes, multidisciplinary team care, geriatrics, patient education and self-management, and cultural competence.

- *Information Technology.* More sophisticated information technology is required to provide high-quality, coordinated care to those with complex or serious medical conditions. More sophisticated information systems are needed to support efforts to monitor, analyze, and improve patient care. Continued development of electronic medical records will be an important factor in ensuring that all health care organizations and providers involved in the care of a patient have timely access to complete information on the patient's clinical conditions, diagnostic and therapeutic test results, and services received. Confidentiality protections must be respected throughout the process of technology development.

- *Regulatory Framework.* Developing a regulatory approach for the Medicare+Choice program that affords adequate protections for beneficiaries with serious and complex medical conditions while encouraging innovation in a rapidly changing health care environment will be an ongoing challenge. Periodic evaluation and modification will be essential.

- *Applied Research.* Research is needed to further inform the policy process and to identify best practices in the care of patients with serious and complex conditions. Attention should be focused on the following areas: effects of benefits coverage and payment methods on care delivery; determination and dissemination of best practices in the identification of patients with serious and complex conditions; efficacy, effectiveness, and efficiency of multidisciplinary teams; use of information technology to support care coordination and delivery; and development of innovative methods of designing, implementing, and coordinating medical, social, and other services.

These and related issues will require HCFA to actively collaborate with all types of payors, health care plans, providers, research organizations, and consumer and disability groups to develop strategies and solutions that will maximize the quality of health care and other services for patients with serious and complex medical conditions.

CONCLUSIONS

The needs of patients with serious and complex medical conditions far exceed the boundaries of a single issue such as access to specialists for care. For health care delivery systems to provide high-quality, effective care for these patients, the systems must be responsive to a diverse array of clinical, social, mental, and functional health issues. The health care delivery system must also be capable of working effectively with other community and social support systems.

The questions raised by HCFA concerning implementation and regulations for the Medicare+Choice program apply broadly to include all health care delivery and payment systems, including fee-for-service systems. This study is one of the first to address these complex and extremely important topics. Thus, the committee urges HCFA, health care plans, and consumer groups to view this report, and especially its conclusions and recommendations, as first steps in the effort to address the unique and complicated needs of persons with serious and complex medical conditions and to ensure that they receive the most cost-effective and best-quality care. The work of this committee is intended to support and provide direction for future work to be conducted by HCFA, in collaboration with all types of health care plans and consumer organizations, to design innovative strategies to ensure adequate reimbursement, access to broad care management, and the highest possible quality of treatment services required by patients with serious and complex medical conditions.

1

Introduction

CHARGE TO THE INSTITUTE OF MEDICINE

The definition of health has evolved over time from an emphasis on mortality and survival rates to a multidimensional perspective that includes "an emphasis on the individual's ability to perform daily activities, and . . . an emphasis on positive themes of happiness, social and emotional well-being, and quality of life" (McDowell and Newell, 1996). Similarly, the World Health Organization has updated its definition to emphasize the role of health as a resource for living that applies to individuals, groups, communities, or whole populations. Specifically, the current World Health Organization definition asserts that "for people to reach a state of complete physical, mental, and social well-being, an individual or group must be able to identify and realize aspirations, to satisfy needs, and to change or cope with the environment" (World Health Organization, 1986).

As the paradigm for health has shifted away from acute care interventions and reducing deaths, a model to address serious and complex medical conditions has emerged. Such conditions are frequently persistent in nature and require intermittent interventions to proactively identify and resolve emerging problems and resolve acute exacerbations of illness or disability. There is also a need for coordination of medical and other services to support and sustain individuals' functional ability, as well as their physical, social, and mental health and well-being.

To help provide a framework for the committee's deliberations, a paper was commissioned from David R. Nerenz, Ph.D., director of the Centers for Health Services Research, Henry Ford Health System, Detroit. This paper addressed alternative definitions for serious and complex conditions and is included in this chapter.

Frequently, a complex and comprehensive array of medical and other services is required to manage the multidimensional sequelae of populations with serious or complex medical conditions. Interventions are required not only to respond to the most immediate and acute threats to physical well-being, but also to prevent further complications and to initiate and sustain improvements in overall quality of life. Efforts to accomplish the latter require systems and services to address the long-term physical, social, and mental dimensions included in currently accepted definitions of health.

The nation's health care delivery system has been challenged to accommodate the unique and complicated needs of the growing numbers of Americans with serious or complex medical conditions. Of particular concern are strategies to finance the long-term provision of complicated arrays of health and other services required by these patients. Issues have also arisen about ensuring access to care and quality of care for the growing numbers of individuals with persistent, disabling, or progressively life-threatening medical conditions. Federal health care programs (Medicare and Medicaid) share concerns about these issues with health care plans—including health maintenance organizations, other types of managed care plans, and fee-for-service plans—and a broad constituency of consumers including persons with disabilities.

A leading initiative to address quality of care and access to care issues has been the President's Advisory Commission on Consumer Protection and Quality in the Health Care Industry. One aspect of the commission's work has been development of a Consumers' Bill of Rights and Responsibilities (President's Advisory Commission, 1998a). Of particular relevance to consumers with serious, complex, persistent, disabling, or progressively life-threatening medical conditions is the right to select providers and health care plans that will ensure access to appropriate high-quality health care. Specifically, the Consumers' Bill of Rights and Responsibilities states that "consumers with complex or serious medical conditions who require frequent specialty care should have direct access to a qualified specialist of their choice within a plan's network of providers. Authorization, when required, should be for an adequate number of direct access visits under an approved treatment plan" (President's Advisory Commission, 1998b).

Coincident with the activities of the President's Advisory Commission on Consumer Protection and Quality in the Health Care Industry, the Balanced Budget Act of 1997, Title IV, was passed with implications for Medicare, Medicaid, and Children's Health Provisions (Public Law 105-33, August 5, 1997). A major implication of the Balanced Budget Act of 1997 was the development of a new health care plan for Medicare beneficiaries called Medicare+Choice. According to the interim final regulations for the establishment of the Medicare+Choice program, Section 422.112 addressed issues concerning patient access to services. Specifically, it states that plans must have procedures approved by HCFA for:

1. identification of individuals with serious or complex medical conditions;

INTRODUCTION

2. assessment of these conditions, including medical procedures to diagnose and monitor them on an ongoing basis; and

3. establishment and implementation of a treatment plan appropriate to these conditions, with an adequate number of direct access visits to specialists to accommodate the treatment plan. Treatment plans must be time-specific and updated periodically by the primary care provider.

In response to a request by HCFA, the Institute of Medicine proposed a study to examine definitions of serious and complex medical conditions and related issues. Specific elements of the charge to the Institute of Medicine are:

1. Should health plans be required to have a general policy for dealing with serious or complex medical conditions, or should HCFA provide more specific guidance as to the types of beneficiaries to be included in this requirement?

2. If specific guidance is to be provided by HCFA, what are the advantages and disadvantages of alternative measurement approaches (e.g., activities of daily living scales, listing of medical conditions)? How feasible would it be for plans to implement such guidance about specific measurement approaches? Should the need for coordination with community and social service agencies be included in the definition of "complex conditions"?

3. What are the implications of alternative definitions for Medicaid and commercial programs, when applied to Medicare beneficiaries who are dual eligible?

Consideration of these issues demonstrated unequivocally to the committee the challenges of caring for highly vulnerable populations such as those having serious and complex medical conditions. The challenges ranged from ensuring quality, coordination, and continuity of care for these patient populations from a wide variety of service providers to clarifying issues associated with access to specialty care, patient confidentiality, patients' right to choice and involvement in their health care, provider and plan liability, and appeal and grievance processes.

SCOPE AND ORGANIZATION OF THIS REPORT

In the remainder of Chapter 1, alternative operational definitions of "serious and complex" medical conditions are examined, including discussions of their relative strengths and weaknesses. Chapter 2 outlines the challenges of ensuring timely access to high-quality health care services and resources for patients with serious and complex medical conditions. Chapter 3 presents the committee's overarching conclusions and recommendations in response to specific elements of the charge. Together, these chapters suggest an approach to understanding the implications of defining serious and complex medical conditions for managed care and other types of health plans and make recommendations in eight areas. Finally, there are five appendixes to this report. Appendix A provides a summary of the workshop proceedings. Appendixes B, C, and D, respectively, include brief biographical sketches of the workshop panel members, the workshop agenda, and a list of workshop participants. Appendix E contains brief biographical sketches for each of the seven members of the committee.

DEFINITIONS OF SERIOUS AND COMPLEX MEDICAL CONDITIONS: ALTERNATIVES AND IMPLICATIONS

Background

Managed care has the potential to significantly improve the quality of health care provided to health plan members. The original promise embodied in the term "health maintenance organization" was an emphasis on preventive services, early detection of illness, close coordination of medical and nonmedical health services, and treatment care plans designed to maintain function and minimize disability. For some enrollees and in some plans, this potential has been realized. In the best of circumstances, a fragmented, uncoordinated set of services has been replaced by a more seamless array of services tailored to the needs, values, and priorities of plan members.

There is another side to managed care, though. For members in some plans, managed care seems to mean a system of hurdles, hoops, and barriers that prevent access to needed services. This side of managed care is the one that has frequently been portrayed in print and electronic media and has captured the attention of politicians and patient advocates who are working on a number of patient protection initiatives.

Access to care can be a significant issue for anyone with an illness, but it is particularly significant for those individuals who have conditions with the potential to cause death, disability, or serious discomfort unless treated with the best available technologies. Access to specialty care or to specific treatment or diagnostic services can become literally an issue of life or death for people with cancer, heart disease, HIV/AIDS, and a number of other acute and persistent conditions.

With these considerations in mind, the President's Commission on Consumer Protection and Quality in the Health Care Industry raised the question of whether patients with serious and complex medical conditions should have a guarantee of direct access to qualified specialists within their plan's network of providers (President's Advisory Commission, 1998b). The Health Care Financing Administration has been charged with developing regulations for Medicare+Choice plans that would implement such a guarantee.

Any such provision written into federal or state law or into the accreditation process for health plans would require a clear, practical definition of the term *serious and complex medical condition*. The remainder of this chapter outlines conceptual categories of conditions that might be considered serious and complex, examines possible alternative operational definitions to screen for the presence of serious and complex conditions, and discusses the implications of these definitions for use in the regulatory or legislative process.

Conceptual Overview—Serious and Complex Conditions

A number of criteria can be used to describe medical conditions as "serious and complex." These could include severity of the illness, degree of impairment or disability, and level of need for comprehensive care management. Disability is defined according to the Americans with Disabilities Act (1990) as pertaining to persons with a physical or mental impairment that substantially limits a "major life activity," persons with a record of such an impairment, or persons who believe that others regard them as having such an impairment. The following presents examples descriptive criteria for serious and complex medical conditions. It is important to recognize that these conditions **may** be serious and complex for **some** patients at **some** points during the course of their disease or disability. The conditions will not necessarily be serious and complex for **all** patients at all times. Further the list is intended to suggest criteria for serious and complex conditions but it is not an exhaustive summary of such criteria.

- *Conditions that are life threatening:* (1) cancer, (2) heart disease, (3) stroke, and (4) HIV/AIDS.
- *Conditions that cause serious disability without necessarily being life threatening:* (1) stroke, (2) closed head or spinal cord injuries, (3) mental retardation, and (4) congenital malformations.
- *Conditions that cause significant pain or discomfort that can cause serious interruptions to life activities:* (1) allergies, (2) migraine, (3) arthritis, and (4) sickle cell disease.
- *Conditions that require major commitments of time and effort from caregivers for a substantial period of time:* (1) mobility disorders, (2) blindness, (3) Alzheimer's disease and other dementias, (4) chronic obstructive pulmonary disease, (5) paraplegia or quadriplegia, (6) Down's syndrome, and (7) depression.
- *Conditions that may require frequent monitoring:* (1) diabetes, (2) conditions requiring anticoagulation treatment, (3) severe asthma, (4) severe allergies, and (5) schizophrenia and other psychotic illnesses.
- *Conditions that predict or are associated with severe consequences:* (1) hypertension (associated with heart disease), (2) depression (associated with suicide), (3) diabetes (associated with blindness, kidney failure), and (4) alcohol and other substance abuse (associated with intentional and unintentional injuries).
- *Conditions associated with negative consequences for someone else:* (1) high-risk pregnancy (risk to newborn), (2) HIV/AIDS (risk to sex partner), and (3) tuberculosis (risk to community in general).
- *Conditions that affect multiple organ systems:* (1) HIV/AIDS, (2) cancer, and (3) diabetes.

- *Conditions that require management to "tight" physiological parameters:* (1) conditions requiring anticoagulation therapy, (2) type I diabetes (possibly type II also), and (3) kidney failure.
- *Conditions whose management requires coordination of multiple specialties:* (1) breast cancer, (2) depression comorbid with serious medical conditions, (3) multiple sclerosis, and (4) cerebral palsy.
- *Conditions whose treatment carries a risk of serious complications:* (1) most cancers, and (2) other conditions requiring complex surgery.
- *Conditions requiring adjustment in a "nonmedical environment":* (1) mobility disorders, (2) blindness and other sensory disorders, (3) Alzheimer's disease, and (4) frailty.

These categories are not mutually exclusive, and clinical conditions such as cancer can appear under several headings. Serious and complex medical conditions should reflect the characteristics of the management of the condition rather than some inherent biological complexity. Although there may be some correlation between biological parameters and complexity of management, it is possible to imagine biologically complex conditions that are easy to treat because a very simple treatment (e.g., a once-a-day prescription drug) has been proven effective. Alternatively, some biologically simple conditions (e.g., spinal cord injuries) may be very complex from a management point of view. In this report, the various meanings of serious and complex will have more to do with illness and disability management than with underlying biology.

Potential Operational Definitions and Criteria

None of the above concepts is of sufficient specificity to be used to write or implement regulations about serious and complex medical conditions. They may, however, represent a set of screens to assess whether potential operational definitions are sufficiently inclusive of the range of conditions that might fit in the category of serious and complex medical conditions. A number of possible operational definitions for serious and complex conditions are described below, along with a summary of their strengths and weaknesses related to validity, reliability, and feasibility. Comments on strengths and weaknesses are not meant to be definitive but to highlight points for further consideration.

Disease Code Definitions

ICD-9 Codes Alone. The five-digit *International Classification of Diseases, Ninth and Tenth Editions* (ICD-9 or ICD-10) coding system would permit the classification of individual diseases or codes (down to the fifth-digit level if necessary) as either being or not being serious and complex medical conditions (American Medical Association, 1999). Using a set of conceptual criteria like those presented at the beginning of this chapter, expert panels could make such determinations, perhaps requiring an additional factor to be added to the codes when the codes themselves are ambiguous relative to a description of serious and complex medical conditions. In practice, then, an individual with one or more ICD-9 codes in the "included" list in a defined period would be considered to have a serious and complex medical condition. The codes would typically be found in insurance claims databases. Most managed care plans would be able to use a "presence-of-codes" rule to identify patients with serious and complex conditions.

Strengths. Rules would be clear and obvious to patients, physicians, health plan representatives, and external regulators. Data would be fairly readily available in existing administrative data sources. Rules could be revised and updated easily since no fundamental changes in data collection or coding technology would be required for changes.

Weaknesses. There would be a clear incentive for "gaming" or "upcoding" and "downcoding" in ambiguous situations in which one code would qualify as a serious and complex medical condition and another potentially valid code would not. Using ICD-9 codes alone fails to capture the severity of disease. Moreover, they do not address the issue of comorbid conditions. Coding may be biased or inaccurate.

ICD-9 Codes Plus Severity Codes. For some ICD-9 codes, a fifth digit is interpretable as a "severity" code. Future enhancements of coding systems in either inpatient or outpatient systems may involve the use of a fifth digit or some other convention to indicate a severity or complexity level within the basic disease code. Classification of conditions as serious and complex would then depend on both the ICD-9 or -10 "stem" and the severity code attached to it.

Strengths. The system would carry most of the advantages of ICD-9 disease codes alone and add the precision of a severity level that would serve to make finer distinctions possible for conditions such as diabetes, asthma, or hypertension.

Weaknesses. Unless the clinical criteria for various severity codes are very clearly and objectively defined, there will be an incentive for either upcoding or downcoding distortion in the severity field. It may be very difficult to audit or validate such codes without clear, objective definitions. Health plans wishing to avoid the provision of additional services may implement procedures designed to make providers use the lowest possible severity codes. Use of ICD-9 or -10 codes with severity codes will not address the issues of comorbidity, coding errors, and coding biases.

DSM-IV Codes. For mental health and substance abuse conditions, psychiatrists may prefer the use of *Diagnostic and Statistical Manual for Mental Disorders* (Fourth Edition) codes to ICD-9 or -10 codes (American Psychiatric Association, 1994). The DSM-IV classification system may permit a finer-grained distinction among types of condition and severity level. Use of these codes would also require some sort of expert panel process to determine which codes or categories should be associated with regulations about serious and complex medical conditions.

Strengths. Some of the same advantages would be found here as with the ICD-9 codes. Once established, the rules would be clear to virtually all parties involved. The coding system is generally well established among mental health and substance abuse providers and would be familiar to those most likely to be assigning codes to individual patients.

Weaknesses. The DSM-IV system is not typically used in insurance claims due to concerns about confidentiality; it is therefore much less likely than the ICD-9 system to be feasible to implement from the claims databases of health care plans. Use of the system may require manual medical record abstraction, which would make it extremely expensive and also presents possible compromises to confidentiality. Furthermore, the DSM-IV is applicable only to mental health and substance abuse care.

International Classification of Impairments, Activities, and Participation (ICIDH-2). This classification system is similar to the ICD-9 system in that it seeks to provide a standard terminology for use in describing specific patient characteristics and is supported by the World Health Organization (World Health Organization, 1997). The difference is the subject matter. Whereas ICD-9 and -10 focus on diseases or injuries, ICIDH-2 focuses on impairments; the acronym reflects the original system's use of the terms disabilities and handicaps. In the present context, individuals having specific impairments would be considered to have serious and complex medical conditions.

Strengths. The ICIDH-2 system provides a standard nomenclature and typology for the entire range of impairments and disabilities. To the extent that any of these specific problems are valid markers of serious and complex medical conditions, the ICIDH-2 system provides a clear way of assigning codes to the impairments to facilitate accurate classification. The ICIDH-2 system may represent some disabilities better than do current ICD-9 codes.

Weaknesses. The ICIDH-2 system is not nearly as well known or widely used in the United States as the ICD-9 system. It has not been linked to reimbursement by public or private payors, and it has not served as the basis for other well-known patient classification systems (e.g., ICD-9 codes have been used to build diagnosis-related groups). There is really no infrastructure in place to support the use of this system, even if there are clear matches between specific ICIDH-2 codes and the concept of serious and complex medical conditions.

Functional Status Definitions

Karnofsky Performance Status. The Karnofsky scale is one of the oldest functional status measures in use today (Karnofsky and Burchenal, 1949). It is a single 0–100 scale (generally used in increments of 10 for individuals) used to describe patients' functional ability. Individuals at the low ranges of the scale are presumably there because of some serious medical condition, although the scale does not strictly require that there be a distinct medical reason for a given level of function. In the context of describing serious and complex medical conditions, a threshold (or possibly multiple thresholds for different ages or classes of patients) would need to be established.

Strengths. The Karnofsky scale is generally well known and accepted in a variety of clinical areas, particularly oncology. Although there may be some potential for gaming, the definitions for various levels of the scale provide some opportunity for validation or auditing.

Weaknesses. This scale is not typically found in administrative databases and is not often used to describe patients outside of research contexts or specific clinical areas (e.g., oncology) in which it has come into common use. Although the scale in general has proven validity, the assignment of an individual to one of two or three adjacent levels can be somewhat arbitrary. If being described as having a serious and complex medical condition depended on being below a certain threshold, there could be an incentive to put a patient either above or below the threshold that would bias "gray area" cases.

Another key problem is that the scale does not directly refer to any specific medical condition, so a serious and complex medical condition is evident only indirectly in the scale score. This approach may be useful only if combined with some more explicit coding of disease states (e.g., some cancer patients with Karnofsky scores of <50 may be judged to have a serious and complex medical condition, whereas not all cancer patients or all patients with Karnofsky scores of <50 would be so labeled). In addition, individual scores may not be stable over the period required to gather data, assemble a database, and determine eligibility for individual patients.

SF-36, SF-12, or Similar "Profile" Scales. Scales such as the Short Form-36 (SF-36), Short Form-12 (SF-12), Dartmouth COOP Chart, and so forth, are similar to the Karnofsky scale in that they assign numbers to individuals to reflect varying levels of functional status or health-related quality of life (Ware and Sherbourne, 1992). The scales differ in that they contain two or more specific dimensions on which individuals receive scores. It is possible, then, to select specific dimensions rather than an overall score, or perhaps to identify a specific profile of scores that would be consistent with the concept of a serious and complex medical condition. Again, the scores do not reflect the presence of any specific medical condition. Most of the scales are designed to apply to patients with any medical condition or with no condition at all.

Strengths. The SF-36 and SF-12 in particular are widely known and used frequently for performance measurement, quality improvement, and research purposes. The scales do not take long to administer. They are becoming more widely used in managed care plans on a full-membership rather than a disease-specific basis. The Health Care Financing Administration already requires this sort of survey in Medicare+Choice plans for "report card" and consumer choice purposes, so plans serving Medicare beneficiaries are familiar with these instruments.

Weaknesses. Most of the concerns about the use of the Karnofsky scale apply to these other scales as well. In addition, the scales are almost always completed on a self-report basis, so patients must be engaged in the process of data collection. The Karnofsky scale, by contrast, is based on clinician evaluation and is easier to incorporate into a claims-based data collection process. Scale scores in and of themselves do not identify serious and complex medical conditions, but the scale scores used in combination with other information (e.g., ICD-9 codes in claims databases) might add precision to the classification process.

Quality of Well-Being, Health Utilities Index, or Similar Utility-Based Scales.
A number of scales are designed to evaluate individual patients' health status on a scale from 0 to 1, where 0 is death or the worst imaginable health status and 1 represents full function and absence of any pain or disability (Kaplan et al., 1989; Torrance, 1987). The purpose of this particular scaling format is to permit the calculation of quality-adjusted life years (QALYs) or disability-adjusted life years (DALYs) that adjust the value of a year of life according to the quality of life reflected in the 0–1 scale. A year at a level of 1 is worth 1; a year at a level of .4 is worth .4, or is equivalent to .4 of a year at level 1. These scale scores would presumably be used in the same way as the Karnofsky, SF-36, or other scores. Individuals below a certain defined threshold would be considered to have (or at least be likely to have) a serious and complex medical condition.

Strengths. Scaling is similar to the Karnofsky in that it is a single dimension with intuitively interpretable values. The translation of 0–1 scores into QALYs, DALYs, and similar measures may allow the incorporation of life expectancy or life expectancy without disability into the calculation of serious and complex medical conditions.

Weaknesses. Most of the same objections to functional status scores listed above apply here as well. The scores may not be stable over long periods of time for specific individuals with serious and complex conditions. The scores do not directly reflect the presence of any specific medical condition, and they may be subject to gaming if the underlying data collection methods permit it. The Quality of Well-Being scale requires patients to answer approximately 40 questions; other scales such as the Euro-Qol scale involve as few as 5 items. In any case, however, the direct involvement of patients is required for data collection.

ADL or IADL Scales. Activities of daily living (ADLs) or instrumental activities of daily living (IADLs) involve the assessment of patients' ability to perform defined tasks (e.g., getting dressed, bathing, using a telephone) (Katz et al., 1963; Lawton and Brody, 1969). The items are somewhat more specific than those involved in some of the functional status scales described above, but the intent of scaling is similar—to classify or score individuals according to their level of function or independence. In determining eligibility for some disability benefit programs, ADL or IADL scores are expressed in terms such as "limited in two or more areas," so that the issue is not the overall score but the number of areas of impairment.

Strengths. There is some precedent for using ADLs and IADLs as criteria for determining eligibility for specific benefits or services (e.g., long-term-care services). The criteria are reasonably well defined, and there is a long history of use of the scales for research and clinical purposes.

Weaknesses. As with other functional status measures, ADLs and IADLs do not directly indicate the presence of a serious and complex medical condition although individuals with severe ADL or IADL limitations may have such conditions. Alternatively, patients with a low number of limitations on these measures may also have a serious and complex medical condition. The ADLs or IADLs are used in the context of care management programs, rehabilitation programs, or long-term-care programs, but they are not typically used more broadly among the general population of health plan members. Some method of data collection would have to be developed for large numbers of patients who are not currently assessed.

Patient Classification System Definitions

DRGs. Diagnosis-related groups (DRGs) are familiar to most plans and providers as the basis for payment to hospitals by Medicare and many other public and private payors. The DRGs were designed to group patients together who are similar in terms of length of stay and other measures of resource consumption in the inpatient setting. The "D" in DRGs indicates that the system is based on ICD-9 diagnostic codes, but information on age, surgical procedures, and complications or comorbidities is also used to assign patients to DRGs for payment purposes. The DRGs could conceivably be used as a means of determining whether patients have serious and complex medical conditions, and the information beyond diagnostic code may provide a more precise classification than diagnosis alone. Presumably, a diagnosis with complications or comorbidities is inherently more serious and complex than one without them.

Strengths. The DRG system is essentially universal in acute care medical and surgical hospitals and may be applicable to some psychiatric, substance abuse, rehabilitation, or long-term-care facilities. Because the system is used for payment purposes, there is a means available for auditing DRG coding to prevent most intentional gaming. The DRG information is contained in virtually all administrative databases on inpatient care.

Weaknesses. The DRG system is a population-based measure of very general categories and is not applicable to any specific individual. The system is not useful for patients who have not been admitted to a hospital. It may be possible to map a set of ICD-9 codes used in outpatient settings to the algorithms used to assign DRGs from inpatient codes, but it is not clear that the diagnoses associated with long lengths of stay or high resource use in the inpatient setting are necessarily serious and complex in the outpatient setting. Since most health plan members at any specific time are not admitted to a hospital, no DRG information would be readily available for most plan members at any particular time. Likewise, persons with serious and complex medical conditions that are managed successfully on an outpatient basis would not have any DRG information available.

DCGs. Diagnostic cost groups (DCGs) are an alternative set of patient groupings (Ash et al., 1989; Ellis et al., 1996; Lamers, 1999). In this case, the goal is to classify patients together who are similar in terms of annual expenditures across all settings rather than length of stay or expenditure in just the inpatient setting. The original DCG modeling was based on inpatient diagnoses, but subsequent versions have incorporated both inpatient and outpatient diagnoses in model development. The DCGs would be useful only to the extent that annual expense is associated with the concept of serious and complex medical conditions.

Strengths. The DCGs have been well researched since the mid-1980s and are beginning to be used in prominent applications. For example, HCFA has decided to use DCGs—albeit for inpatient services only—to implement provisions of the 1997 Balanced Budget Act regarding risk-adjusted capitation payments to Medicare+Choice plans. Some large private employers (e.g., Ford Motor Company) are beginning to use DCGs in the analysis of health care costs and quality for their employees. The grouping algorithms use generally available administrative data that plans have in their billing or encounter data systems. The DCG system has "face validity" for the current application to the extent that users accept an association between the categories of serious and complex medical conditions and annual expenditures.

Weaknesses. The DCG system was designed for a specific purpose—to model annual expenses based on diagnoses—and this purpose may not exactly match the description of persons with serious and complex medical conditions. If there are conditions that are not expensive but are very serious, or conditions that are expensive but not serious in any other sense, then the DCG system would yield misleading results. It has also been noted that the DCG system can reward inefficient patient management because of its assumption that higher costs are associated with greater complexity of care. Such higher costs could, in fact, be the result of inefficient management. Although HCFA has made a commitment to use the system for Medicare+Choice plans, it is not widely used in other settings for risk-adjusting capitation payments to plans.

ACGs. Ambulatory care groups (ACGs) are similar to DCGs in that they are designed to group patients together who are similar on a measure of annual cost or expenditure (Weiner et al., 1991). As the title implies, the focus of ACGs is on outpatient rather than inpatient care, so the system is perhaps better suited to physician profiling or partial capitation payment applications in the outpatient arena than to more global payment applications. The ACGs might conceivably be a better conceptual fit than DCGs to the concept of serious and complex medical conditions. It would be an empirical question whether ACGs or DCGs more accurately predict the need for a broad strategy of care management, as judged by some independent criterion.

Strengths. A number of health plans (the exact number is uncertain and can change frequently) use ACGs for purposes of physician profiling or adjusting capitation payments to individual physicians or physician groups. Most plans would at least be familiar with ACGs and would be able to assign patients to ACGs using data routinely available in administrative or encounter databases.

Weaknesses. Annual expense in the outpatient setting is almost certainly correlated with the underlying descriptions of serious and complex medical conditions, but the relationship is not perfect and there may be some misleading results. Given the relatively small number of ACGs, one could expect some heterogeneity within specific ACGs on the extent to which patients really do have serious and complex conditions.

Kaiser Clinical-Behavioral Classification System. The Kaiser system was developed in the 1960s as part of a program of research on health care utilization in Kaiser's Center for Health Research in Portland (Hurtado and Greenlick, 1971). The system is similar to both DCGs and ACGs in that it tries to categorize patients into groups that are homogeneous on overall resource utilization. Also like ACGs and DCGs, the system is based on diagnostic categories but adds other information that helps create homogeneous and clinically meaningful groups.

Strengths. The Kaiser system is based primarily on diagnostic codes that would typically be found in plans' administrative databases. It was designed for a single managed care plan to explain patterns of utilization within that plan.

Weaknesses. The Kaiser system is not as well known now as the DCG, ACG, or DRG systems and has not been widely used outside Kaiser. Although many of the categories seem to have a conceptual link to categories of serious and complex medical conditions, the system was not designed specifically with this issue in mind. Consequently, it shares many of the same problems as the DCG or ACG systems regarding possible mismatch of concepts.

Utilization Definitions

Total Annual Expenditure or Cost. The classification systems just described (DCGs, ACGs, Kaiser) use annual expense in one way or another to define homogeneous groups. The measure of cost or expense itself could be used to identify a group or groups of persons who are likely to have serious and complex medical conditions. For example, one could apply a screen to identify individuals in the top 5 or 10 percent of annual expenditures in a health plan.

Strengths. Most plans can use existing administrative data sets to identify patients with high absolute or relative expenses in any defined period. The data requirements are less than for the DCG or ACG approaches since diagnosis or procedure code information is not necessary to calculate costs.

Weaknesses. Costs in a previous period do not necessarily predict either future costs or costs associated with current needs for specialty care. Patients with acute injuries who are fully recovered might have needed specialized services at the time of the injury (before they would have been identified in an administrative database due to lag time in claims submission and processing), but would not necessarily need such access in the future if the injuries are fully healed. Expense information might have to be combined with diagnostic or other information to accurately identify patients with serious and complex medical conditions.

Above-Threshold Number of Hospital Admissions per Year. Patients who have multiple hospital admissions in a period of time such as a year are a statistically unusual group and are probably dealing with serious and complex medical conditions. Multiple admissions reflect either persistent conditions under poor control, serious illnesses such as cancer that require frequent admissions for administration of complex treatments, serious anatomical problems that require multiple surgeries, or general frailty.

Strengths. Data needed to assess multiple hospital admissions are usually available in plans' administrative databases. There is generally little ambiguity about the occurrence of an admission, so opportunities for gaming are minimized. The measure might be highly specific in that very few people with multiple admissions would not pass some other test of the presence of a serious and complex medical condition.

Weaknesses. The criterion would not be very sensitive because only a few patients with serious and complex medical conditions would be admitted to hospitals multiple times in a given year. As a stand-alone definition or criterion, multiple admissions would probably not be useful, but its predictive value might increase when combined with diagnostic or other criteria (e.g., patients with type I diabetes and two or more admissions for a diabetes-related diagnosis).

Prior Use of Specialty Care. Provider codes in billing or encounter databases could be used to identify patients who have used specialized services in the recent past. To the extent that prior use can be interpreted as continuing need, previous use of specialists and specialized services could be another indicator of individuals with serious and complex medical conditions.

Strengths. Data are probably readily available, although some provider codes may not accurately reflect the provision of specialized services.

Weaknesses. Past use is not necessarily a marker of current or future need, particularly in situations in which the appropriateness of past use might have been questionable.

Use of Specific Treatments, Procedures, or Services. There are specific tests, treatments, or procedures that may identify persons with serious and complex medical conditions. Hospital and health plan credentialing committees address this issue on an ongoing basis, as individuals or groups seek approval to perform various tests or procedures. To the extent that the rules used to grant privileges and credentials can be generalized across plans and parts of the country, a patient's receipt of specific services (or, more specifically, the projected *future* receipt of such services) could be a criterion for identifying that patient as having a serious and complex condition. Organ transplants, for example, might indicate not only the presence of serious disease in the past but also the continuing need for a broad care management approach and the presence of serious and complex conditions in the future.

Strengths. A number of therapeutic procedures (e.g., organ transplants, bone marrow transplants, "cocktail" treatments for HIV/AIDS) are done only in the presence of serious and complex conditions that can be presumed to continue as long as the patient is alive. This sort of definition or criterion, then, would be highly specific in such cases. Although the intensity of need for care management (and the underlying seriousness and complexity of disease) may diminish over time, it may never go away totally. Procedure codes are readily available in administrative databases since they are used for reimbursement.

Weaknesses. At best, this is a partial solution to the problem of defining serious and complex conditions. Not all conditions are associated with distinct treatments. Any tests or procedures done to detect or rule out disease would not be useful since they may find the absence of serious illness rather than its presence.

Physiological Measure Definitions

Laboratory Test Values. Some inpatient severity of illness systems (e.g., APACHE III) rely on laboratory tests to assess the concept of physiological "derangement" and severity of illness. The models are built on a statistical association between extreme laboratory test values and either risk of mortality or inpatient cost. In the inpatient context, patients with extreme lab values may be considered to have serious and complex medical conditions, although not all values would have this connotation. Some laboratory test results may be interpretable as markers of serious and complex conditions over longer periods of time in the outpatient setting. A high prostate-specific antigen value, for example, may indicate the presence of prostate cancer and the need for a broad care management plan for further diagnostic and treatment purposes far into the future.

Strengths. Test values are quantitative, objective, usually precise and accurate, and generally not subject to gaming. A number of tests are used for the purpose of detecting and monitoring serious and complex conditions, so the presence of an abnormal value has a clear, precise meaning.

Weaknesses. Only a fraction of all serious and complex medical conditions can be identified by specific lab tests. Most of the mental health domain would be excluded from this criterion, and there would be major debate about the interpretation of lab tests for other common conditions. Glycosylated hemoglobin, for example, is the "gold standard" for glycemic control in diabetics, but it is not clear that a specific value or range of values would indicate "serious and complex" diabetes rather than some alternative. Plans would have to develop methods of obtaining actual lab test values rather than administrative data on whether a test was done or not.

Other Physical Exam Values (e.g., blood pressure, weight). This set of criteria is conceptually similar to the lab values just discussed. There are some widely used clinical measures that may be markers for the presence of serious and complex medical conditions. Hypertension is identified through blood pressure readings, and unusually high readings could be used as markers of serious and complex hypertension. Weight is a measure of obesity (one might prefer to use body mass index instead), and again, unusually high values might reflect more serious and complex conditions.

Strengths. Measures such as weight, blood pressure, visual acuity, and so forth are common in clinical practice, generally accurate, inexpensive to obtain, and reasonably well interpreted as markers of serious and complex conditions in defined contexts. These measures may be particularly useful in identifying persons with comorbid conditions.

Weaknesses. Health plans do not have this information routinely available in administrative databases, and provider groups may not have the information available in electronic form. Although this information is inexpensive to obtain in a clinical context, it may be very expensive to obtain for large numbers of people to ensure proper identification of those with serious and complex medical conditions. There may be some potential for gaming for individuals at or near a threshold value. There is some potential for misinterpretation of almost all measures especially for those individuals with significant comorbidities.

OASIS-B. The Medicare Home Health Care Quality Assurance and Improvement Demonstration Outcome and Assessment Information Set (OASIS-B) data set has been designed for HCFA to use in monitoring physiological parameters of patients enrolled in home health care programs. While its primary purpose is to assist in stratifying populations by morbidity to set prospective payment rates, this instrument is also expected to be used for quality improvement and other functions. It contains fields to collect a primary and up to five secondary diagnoses, with each entity rated on a 0 through 4 severity scale. It catalogues areas such as prognosis, living arrangements, supportive assistance, sensory status, activities of daily living, and use of medications.

Strengths. This data instrument is used fairly extensively and directly addresses issues concerned with the identification of patients with serious and complex medical conditions. The use of a severity rating scale for each diagnosis coupled with an assessment of functional status and the cataloging of physiological dysfunctions could be very useful in identifying and tracking the progress of individuals with serious and complex conditions.

Weaknesses. This instrument is time intensive to administer and is now mandated for use only in the home health arena. The accuracy of the information when collected in community settings is unknown. There is little experience at this point with systematic use of these data to manage populations of patients and potential impact upon their physiological and functional status.

Care Management Guidelines or Other Entitlement Program Definitions

Eligibility for Medical Disability Payments. Individuals who are eligible for disability payments or related services through private employers, Medicaid programs, Veterans Administration programs, or other public programs may already have had to demonstrate the presence of serious and complex medical conditions. Children eligible for Medicaid benefits through the Children with Special Health Care Needs program, for example, may not need to pass any other tests to be labeled as having a serious and complex medical condition.

Strengths. As long as the criteria and definitions fit, the work of data collection and the use of data to classify individuals have already been done. No separate process has to be invented or used.

Weaknesses. As indicated above in the discussion of ADLs and IADLs, disability per se does not necessarily indicate the presence of a serious and complex medical condition.

NHO Guidelines. The National Hospice Organization (NHO) has disseminated a set of guidelines for appropriateness of hospice care (National Hospice Organization, 1996). These guidelines have been used to make decisions about the care of individual patients to judge their appropriateness for the hospice benefit in Medicare. The guidelines are based on combinations of diagnostic, functional, lab test, and other criteria the underlying concept of which is the likelihood of death in a period of 6 months or less. Virtually all patients meeting the NHO guidelines would be considered to have a serious and complex condition.

Strengths. This is a criterion with very high specificity. People meeting the NHO guidelines clearly have serious and complex conditions.

Weaknesses. The NHO guidelines affect only those people with terminal illnesses, who make up only a small subset of those in the health plan population with serious and complex conditions. Even where the guidelines are used, they are not generally found in administrative databases because they do not produce a single score that can be entered and stored readily.

Combined Definitions

There is no reason why any of the above definitions would have to be used in isolation. In fact, the best operational definition (as judged by assessments of "false positives" or "false negatives") would almost certainly be one that combined different types of information to come as close as possible to identifying categories of patients with serious and complex conditions. As long as the necessary data elements were available, relatively sophisticated combination rules could be developed from the above list to create a more precise definition that would minimize both false positives and false negatives. For example, although not all diabetics (ICD-9 codes 250.xx) are necessarily considered to have serious and complex medical conditions, those type I diabetics with one or more early signs of complications (e.g., diabetic retinopathy) might be more appropriately included in this category.

Summary

No single criterion or definition in the above lists will completely meet the needs of HCFA to define patient populations with serious and complex medical conditions. It is almost certain that some sort of combined criteria will have to be developed to reflect underlying medical condition, current disability, severity of a medical condition or disability, and perhaps the presence of a treatment that will continue into the future and that inherently requires access to broad strategies of care management.

It is the opinion of the committee that the state of current clinical and research literature does not yet support the selection of specific categories of patients or service needs to define serious or complex medical conditions. Disease classification systems such as DRGs, DCGs, and ICD-9 lack the sensitivity and specificity required to identify patients with serious and complex medical conditions. The validity of patient classification systems and functional status definitions has yet to be established. Efforts to develop case-mix-adjusted reimbursement systems that ensure cost-effectiveness and high-quality interventions for patients with serious and complex conditions are still in the early stages or are limited to a single disease category. Similarly, efforts to develop standardized protocols for issues of care coordination, continuity of care, care management, and service reimbursement have not met with great success. Furthermore, significant variation on these issues is apparent for different types of health care plans, provider organizations, and patient populations.

Furthermore, several limitations are shared by the suggested list of potential operational definitions for serious and complex medical conditions. First, the measurement of specific dimensions of health and health status will change and improve in the coming years as researchers advance their knowledge about the technologies associated with methods of data collection, management, analysis, and interpretation. Health care plans and HCFA should ensure that state-of-the-art measurement techniques are adapted as quickly as possible to improve identification of patients with serious and complex medical conditions.

It is also important to acknowledge that a system of screening patient populations for the presence of serious or complex conditions will be limited by the frequency with which such assessments are made. Too frequent assessments may not allow sufficient time to elapse for measures to maintain a level of sensitivity to detect change. In contrast, infrequent assessments may fail to detect changes that occur. In either case, patient populations will be at risk of misclassification for having or not having a serious or complex medical condition. Careful consideration must be given to determining the appropriate intervals between identification and screening of patient populations for the presence of a new condition that might be serious and complex, the continuation of an existing serious and complex condition, and the resolution of a condition previously determined to be serious and complex in nature.

Health care plans and HCFA must also be cognizant of the limitations of data that is collected, analyzed, or interpreted retrospectively. Examples of such data might be submission of information about claims and claims resolution data. Reliance on retrospective data may result in significant delays in identifying beneficiaries with serious and complex medical conditions. Furthermore, use of retrospective data to predict future events has the potential for misclassification of patients as having or not having a serious and complex medical condition.

Health plans and HCFA should also be aware of the challenges inherent in the process of data collection, management, analysis, and interpretation. The potential for errors and biases is present at each step and could result in misclassification of patients with serious and complex medical conditions. The collection of timely information that is of sufficient sensitivity and specificity to reduce the number of false-positive and false-negative classifications as serious and complex imposes significant burdens and will require allocation of adequate resources and professionally trained staff.

Clinical research relevant to defining patient populations as having serious and complex conditions and developing the most effective care protocols to respond to patient needs is evolving rapidly, but only preliminary results are available. For example, research in correlating patient volume with patient outcomes, differentiating access to services as a function of health plan benefits, and addressing variations in quality of care has just begun to yield meaningful results about particular groups of patients. The committee anticipates that this research will continue to evolve and will provide more definitive conclusions to guide the efforts of health plans to identify patients with serious and complex medical conditions and ensure appropriate levels of treatment and care management. As the science base is strengthened, so too will be the ability of HCFA and health plans to correctly identify patients with serious and complex medical conditions who would benefit from broad strategies of care management.

2
Challenges in Health Care Delivery for Patients with Serious and Complex Medical Conditions

As the paradigm for health has shifted in focus away from acute care interventions and reducing deaths, a new model of health care delivery has emerged. This model emphasizes the provision of ongoing care to sustain life at the highest level of quality possible, proactive interventions to prevent development of further problems, and intermittent medical interventions to address acute exacerbation of illness and disability. These efforts are accompanied by services to support and sustain individuals' physical, social, and mental health and well-being. As noted by the Institute of Medicine: "To accommodate the changing needs of an increasingly older society we must broaden the traditional goals of health—curing disease and preventing its occurrence—to include preventing the ill from becoming disabled and helping the disabled cope with and prevent further disability" (Institute of Medicine, 1999). Rising health care costs, rising consumer expectations, and national efforts to ensure access to care and improve and sustain the quality of health care in the United States are all contributing factors to the need for changes in the traditional health care delivery system.

This chapter briefly reviews issues considered by the committee to have relevance to implementation of regulations concerning patients with serious and complex medical conditions. An in-depth analysis of these issues is beyond both the charge to this committee and the scope of this report. The committee feels, however, that it is critical to recognize the dual roles of HCFA in implementation of regulations for the Medicare+Choice program. First, HCFA is charged with ensuring that patients with serious and complex medical conditions have access to requisite services that will benefit their overall health, well-being, and quality of life. Second, HCFA must be mindful of the need to regulate the costs of care for this patient population to ensure affordability of the Medicare+Choice program.

QUALITY OF HEALTH CARE

Although financing the expanding health care costs associated with the management of serious and complex medical conditions remains a pressing concern, so too are issues addressing quality of care for the growing numbers of individuals with serious and complex medical conditions. Receipt of high-quality care is essential to sustain or restore the health and functioning of millions of Americans with serious and complex medical conditions. Quality of care has been defined as "the degree to which health services for individuals and populations increase the likelihood of desired health outcomes and are consistent with current professional knowledge" (Institute of Medicine, 1990).

A number of initiatives including the Institute of Medicine's National Roundtable on Health Care Quality and the President's Advisory Commission on Consumer Protection and Quality in the Health Care Industry have focused on major sources of compromise in the quality of care delivered to patients (Institute of Medicine, 1999; President's Advisory Commission, 1998b). Although most Americans receive high-quality health care, a significant number experience substandard care regardless of the type of health care delivery system. Due to the potential for a higher level and frequency of involvement with the health care delivery system, persons with serious and complex conditions could be considered at particular risk for errors in the care delivery process.

Four major categories of errors contributing to substandard health care quality have been identified: (1) avoidable errors; (2) underutilization of services; (3) overuse of services; and (4) errors associated with wide variations in health care practices, including regional and small-area variations. Avoidable errors refer to injuries sustained by patients during the course of their care. Some patients die prematurely as a result of such injuries. Underutilization of health care services has also been cited as a major factor contributing to the delivery of poor-quality health care service that can lead to detrimental outcomes associated with functional status and quality of life and may also result in premature death.

Underutilization occurs when patients fail to receive an intervention whose benefits outweigh its risks. Overuse of health care services can also undermine the quality of care. Specifically, overuse refers to the delivery of a health care intervention with a higher likelihood of risk than potential benefit to patients. Finally, errors associated with variations in health care practices have been noted for different patient populations, health care providers, and health care delivery systems.

Patient Characteristics

A number of studies reveal that characteristics of patient populations are associated with variations in the quality of health care. For example, compromises in care have been noted for the elderly, women, members of racial or ethnic minority groups, and members of low socioeconomic or low educational attainment groups. There is evidence of improved quality of care and better outcomes for patients with active systems of social support and for those who have access to care in urban versus rural settings. Health insurance status has also been cited as a predictor of variations in quality of care, with lack of insurance or inadequate coverage associated with lower quality of care (Aday, 1994; Aday et al., 1993b; Blazer et al., 1995; Brook et al., 1990; Elnicki et al., 1995; Erlich, 1985; Fox and Newacheck, 1990; Frenzen, 1991; Freund and Hurley, 1995; Freund and Lewit, 1993; Gibbons et al., 1991; Hofer and Katz, 1996; Imperiale et al., 1988; Ireys et al., 1996; Lave et al., 1995; Lillie-Blanton et al., 1993, 1996; Newacheck et al., 1996; Riley and Lubitz, 1985, 1986; Rogers, 1993; Rowland and Lyons, 1989; Stano and Folland, 1988; Starfield, 1992; Starfield et al., 1991, 1998; Van Nostrand, 1993; Vayda, 1973; Woolhandler and Himmelstein, 1988).

Provider Characteristics

Characteristics of health care providers have also been identified as predictors of variations in quality of care. Provider gender is associated with differential referral rates for gender-specific screening exams. For example, male providers are less likely than their female counterparts to refer female patients for breast and cervical cancer screening exams. Age of providers and length of time in practice are also associated with delivery of state-of-the-art care to patients, with a slightly decreased likelihood of such care by younger providers with fewer years in practice. In contrast, physicians with board certification in particular areas of specialty care and those affiliated with professional societies demonstrate greater knowledge and more frequent use of practice-based guidelines for primary, secondary, and tertiary prevention when compared to their counterparts who lack board certification or membership in professional societies (Bernard et al., 1990; Bunker, 1970; Cherkin et al., 1987; Eisenberg, 1986; Feinglass et al., 1991; Folland and Stano, 1989, 1990; Forrest and Starfield, 1998; Franks and Dickinson, 1986; Garber et al., 1984; Garg et al., 1979; Gittelsohn and Powe, 1995; Greenfield et al., 1992; Greenwald et al., 1984; Hartley et al., 1987; Horn et al., 1986; Kravitz et al., 1992; Linn et al., 1984; McPherson et al., 1982; Powe et al., 1996; Roos et al., 1986; Sandrick, 1984; Stafford et al., 1999; Starfield et al.,1994; Wennberg, 1984, 1985a, 1985b, 1986; Wennberg and Gittelsohn, 1973; White et al., 1984).

Patient Volume

In recent years, studies have begun to examine the correlation between clinical outcomes and hospital or provider case volume for a variety of medical and surgical procedures. Although additional research is required to increase the general understanding of the relationship between patient volume and outcomes, a number of studies have yielded convincing evidence that high-volume, regional providers can deliver complex care with improved short-term outcomes at lower costs when compared to their low-volume regional counterparts. The majority of these studies have compared mortality and morbidity rates and length of hospital stay between high- and low-volume groups. Lower mortality and morbidity rates have been noted for patients receiving care for a wide variety of conditions, including but not limited to, cancer, hepatic resection, arthroplasty and hip fractures, selected surgical procedures, repair of abdominal aortic aneurysms, repair of congenital cardiac defects, carotid surgery, AIDS, organ transplantation, acute myocardial infarction, and neonatal mortality (Banta and Box, 1991; Banta et al., 1992; Bennett et al., 1989, 1995; Choti et al., 1998; Espehaug et al., 1999; Farley and Ozminkowski, 1992; Hannan, 1991; Hannan et al., 1991, 1994, 1995, 1997a, 1997b, 1998; Hillner and Smith, 1999, Hughes et al., 1987, 1988; Jollis et al., 1994; Kantonen et al., 1998; Lavernia and Guzman, 1995; Luft, 1980; Norton et al., 1998; Phibbs et al., 1996; Phillips et al., 1995; Riley and Lubitz, 1985; Rosenfeld et al., 1987; Sollano et al., 1999; Stone et al., 1992; Thiemann et al., 1999).

Health Care Delivery System

Variations in quality of care have also been attributed to aspects of the health care delivery system such as access to academic centers of tertiary care and single versus multiple specialty practice settings. Delivery of care in academic settings is generally associated with improved quality of care. Similarly, quality of care is better for patients receiving services in a multiple specialty practice environment and from practitioners caring for a high volume of patients with a particular illness.

A recent meta-analysis of evidence comparing the performance of managed care plans with that of fee-for-service plans examined results from 37 peer-reviewed studies (Miller and Luft, 1997). Operationalization of quality-of-care measures included hospital admission rates, patient outcomes, lengths-of-stay, hospital expenditures, use of costly procedures, physician visits, outpatient spending, home health care spending and use, total spending, and enrollee satisfaction. There were equal numbers of statistically significant positive and negative results for managed care plan performance compared with fee-for-service plans. However, there was a lack of consistency in the evidence, and more research will be required before conclusions can be drawn about the relative contributions of source of care and payment to variations in quality of care (Bindman et al., 1996; Bradbury et al., 1991; Fine et al., 1990; Gemson and Elinson, 1986; Geraci et al., 1993; Gonnella et al., 1990; Greenfield et al., 1992; Hawkes, 1989; Hill and Brown, 1990; Hillner and Smith, 1999; Holahan et al., 1998; Horn et al., 1991; Iezzoni et al., 1988, 1991, 1992, 1994b; Institute of Medicine, 1999; Kellie and Kelly, 1991; Knaus et al., 1986, 1993; Lambrew et al., 1996; Miller and Luft, 1997; Naessens et al., 1992; Oleske et al., 1998; Riley et al., 1991, 1993, 1994, 1995; Saag et al., 1998; Shwartz et al., 1996; Silber et al.,

1992; Stano and Folland, 1988; Starfield et al., 1991, 1994; Theimann, 1999; Weiner et al., 1995, 1996b).

The President's Advisory Commission and the Institute of Medicine Roundtable concluded that quality of care varies considerably throughout the United States, with wide variations apparent within and between communities, hospitals, practitioners, patients, health care delivery systems, geographic regions, and health conditions (Institute of Medicine, 1999; President's Advisory Commission, 1998b). Such variation in the quality of health care in America is a major cause of excess morbidity and mortality, as well as a contributing factor to rising health care costs and expenditures. Interventions to improve the overall quality of health care have the potential to save lives, reduce disability, improve quality of life and productivity, and reduce health care spending. Given the potential for higher utilization of services of the traditional and expanded health care delivery system, patients with serious and complex medical conditions could be considered at even greater risk of experiencing poor-quality health care in terms of one or more of the major quality-of-care measures.

ACCESS TO CARE

Of particular relevance to the rising expectations of consumers with serious and complex medical conditions is the right to select providers and health care plans that ensure access to appropriate high-quality health care. Specifically, the Consumers' Bill of Rights and Responsibilities states that "consumers with complex or serious medical conditions who require frequent specialty care should have direct access to a qualified specialist of their choice within a plan's network of providers. Authorization, when required, should be for an adequate number of direct access visits under an approved treatment plan."

The literature relevant to access to care presents a conflicting picture. The past decade has been marked by a significant increase in the number and types of health insurance products available to consumers in most geographic regions. Current options include traditional indemnity plans, health maintenance organizations, preferred provider organizations, and other types of managed care plans with various options concerning benefits, premiums, copayments, and health care delivery systems (President's Advisory Commission, 1998b). These options have prompted a reduction in enrollment in fee-for-service plans from 59 percent of American workers in 1991 to 35 percent in 1995 (Employee Benefits Research Institute, 1997). In 1997, more than 5 million Medicare beneficiaries enrolled in 336 managed care plans, an increase of more than 100 percent over 4 years. Similarly, 35 million Medicaid beneficiaries enrolled in managed care plans during the same interval for an increase of more than 170 percent (President's Advisory Commission, 1998b).

The commission notes, however, that the choice in health insurance products is available largely at the level of the group purchaser rather than the individual consumer. In fact, between 1988 and 1997, the choice of health plan offerings by employers decreased. With respect to consumer preferences for health insurance coverage, the majority prefer a high-cost, broad-benefit options package to a lower-cost option with a more limited range of benefits (Kaiser Family Foundation and the Agency for Health Care Policy and Research, 1996). In the survey issued by Kaiser and the Agency for Health Care Policy and Research, the most frequently stated reason for consumers' preferences for greater choice in physicians and other health care professionals was to "see . . . whatever doctor you think is best qualified to treat a particular medical condition."

Although the literature on access to specialized services is just beginning to develop, there is some evidence to suggest that vulnerable groups such as the nonelderly disabled; the "oldest old" (85 years and older); those with functional impairments; and those in fair, poor, or worsening health are more likely to report problems in accessing the care they need compared to their less vulnerable counterparts (Nelson et al., 1997). Such problems have been shown to occur more frequently for enrollees in health maintenance organizations than for those in fee-for-service plans (Nelson et al., 1997). Similarly, a recent study of populations with low incomes demonstrated that Medicaid beneficiaries enrolled in managed care plans are more likely to have difficulties with access to care than their counterparts who are enrolled in commercial plans or Medicaid fee-for-service plans. The most frequent problems in accessing care are noted among Medicaid managed care enrollees in poor health (Lillie-Blanton and Lyons, 1998). Other studies have shown that Medicare beneficiaries enrolled in health maintenance organizations are more likely to disenroll when they are less healthy as measured by mortality rates, preenrollment health care costs, and self-reported health status (Hill and Brown, 1999; Riley et al., 1991, 1996; Rossiter et al., 1988; Sullivan, 1990).

In contrast, other studies do not yield support for the premise that vulnerable populations have limited access to specialized services, poor service, greater inconvenience in accessing care, and restricted choice of providers (Aday and Andersen, 1981; Aday et al., 1993a; DesHarnais, 1985; Dowd et al., 1992; Fama et al., 1995; Luft and Miller, 1988; Moy and Hogan, 1993; Newhouse, 1994; Schlesinger and Mechanic, 1993). For example, disenrollment rates of Medicare health maintenance organization enrollees were compared between cancer patients and noncancer patients. Overall, cancer patients were no more likely to disenroll than other types of enrollees (Riley et al., 1996). Similarly, analysis of data from the National Health Interview Survey revealed that indemnity plans have an equal number of enrollees with chronic illnesses compared to patients enrolled in health maintenance organizations (Fama et al., 1995).

HEALTH CARE COST CONTAINMENT

The health care industry—especially Medicare, Medicaid, health maintenance organizations, and other managed care organizations—is struggling to respond to the increasing prevalence of persistent and disabling conditions and the cost burden these conditions bring to bear on the health care delivery system. In terms of actual expenditures, HCFA estimates that by the year 2000, health care costs in the United States will exceed $1.6 trillion and will comprise more than 16 percent of the gross national product. It is estimated that fully 80 percent of all medical expenses can be attributed to care for individuals with serious and complex conditions. During the past two decades, significant increases in expenditures have been noted for the two major categories of long-term care, nursing home and home health care. Specifically, annual nursing home care expenditures in 1980 were approximately $20 billion, while home health care expenditures averaged $2 billion. Today, annual costs for nursing home care have increased to $70 billion and for home health care to $25 billion. Similarly, pharmacy drug costs are increasing at a 16 to 18 percent annual inflation rate among Medicare beneficiaries.

Medicare and Medicaid

Medicare has assumed a leading role in responding to the complex care needs of populations with serious and complex medical conditions. Similarly, Medicaid has stepped in to meet the needs of children, economically disadvantaged populations, and persons with disabilities who have serious and complex medical conditions. Although Medicare was first designed as a benefit to provide acute care services, a number of factors have contributed to its emergence as a provider of health care services associated with persistent illness, disability, and long-term care. These include advances in medical technology, consumer preferences, policy changes, and the development of a "post-acute care industry," which has expanded Medicare benefits to include skilled nursing facility services, home health services, rehabilitation therapies, hospice care, and durable medical equipment (Ash et al., 1989; Dowd et al., 1992; Lubitz and Riley, 1993; Maguire et al., 1998; Riley and Lubitz, 1989; Riley et al., 1986, 1987).

Medicaid has long been the primary source of public funding for long-term-care interventions. Medicaid reimbursements include nursing home care, intermediate care facilities for persons with mental retardation, home health care, personal care, and home- and community-based services. Medicaid also assumes financial responsibility for reimbursement of both acute and long-term health care services required by persons with disabilities. For example, in 1992, 59 percent of Medicaid spending was directed toward long-term care for the elderly, while 36 and 5 percent, respectively, covered long-term-care services for younger adults and children. In 1993, Medicaid expenditures on home health care and home- and community-based services exceeded $4.5 billion, 10 times the amount spent on home care in 1980 (Freund and Hurley, 1995; Freund and Lewit, 1993; Holahan et al., 1998; Oleske et al., 1998).

Utilization Review and Management

Strategies for cost containment include utilization management and the development of peer review organizations, which attempt to ensure that a comprehensive array of medical services are available when needed while limiting the expenditure of resources for unnecessary and inappropriate medical services. The Institute of Medicine Committee on Utilization Management by Third Parties defines utilization management "as a set of techniques used by or on behalf of purchasers of health benefits to manage health care costs by influencing patient care decision-making through case-by-case assessments of the appropriateness of care prior to its provision" (Institute of Medicine, 1989). Utilization review or management focuses on a single episode of an illness, examines a large number of patients at a low level of intensity, and relies on prior authorization, concurrent review, and retrospective review to evaluate medical necessity (Kellie and Kelly, 1991).

Care Management

Alternatively, some managed care plans have begun to develop comprehensive, integrated service delivery systems such as care management for individuals with persistent, disabling, or progressively life-threatening conditions. Care management has been defined as "a collaborative process which assesses, plans, implements, coordinates, monitors, and evaluates options and services to meet an individual's health needs through communication and available resources to promote quality, cost-effective outcomes" (Case Management Society of America, 1996). Unlike utilization review, care management is proactive in its efforts to identify patients at risk for exacerbation of an illness or disability. Care management focuses on the continuum of care, addresses the needs of a small number of patients, and emphasizes medically appropriate care. Care management plans are intended to ensure better integration of health care service delivery (including social and mental health services, if necessary), minimize duplication of services, and increase the likelihood of proactive identification of costly problems that might arise in the future.

Screening and Risk Assessment

A third effort by plans to deal with rising health care costs and the increasing numbers of individuals with serious and complex conditions focuses on screening and risk assessment. This approach relies on the assessment of interrelationships among the biological, environmental, and behavioral factors considered to be associated with elevated risk for specific health outcomes and increased need for special or intensive therapies. Individuals identified at higher risk for negative physical, social, or mental outcomes can receive interventions earlier in an effort to prevent such outcomes. Such preventive interventions can help reduce overall costs of care and can result in significant improvements in health status and quality of life. Relevant dimensions of risk include age; gender; acute clinical stability; principal diagnosis; severity of principal diagnosis; extent and severity of comorbidities; physical functional status; psychological, cognitive, and psychosocial functioning; cultural, ethnic, and socioeconomic attributes and behaviors; health status and quality of life; and patient attitudes and preferences for outcomes (Ellis et al., 1996; Iezzoni et al., 1988, 1991, 1992, 1994a, 1994b; Naessens et al., 1992; Weiner et al., 1996a).

Alternative Strategies for Cost Containment

Other efforts are underway to control health care costs for patients with serious and complex conditions while ensuring appropriate access to necessary services. For example, disease management programs and multidisciplinary teams for care management are used with increasing frequency to improve the efficiency and coordination of care for patients with serious and complex medical conditions. Efforts are also being made to better manage health care costs while ensuring access to quality services through the use of nurses, nurse specialists, and social workers to manage routine health care and respond to needs for ancillary services.

It is evident from these brief reviews of literature relevant to health care quality and health care cost containment that the relationships among quality of health care, access to care, types of insurance coverage, and serious and complex medical conditions are only beginning to emerge. A great deal of further study will be necessary for any conclusions to be drawn about issues such as access to specialty care, quality of health care, insurance preferences, insurance options, and disenrollment in plans for patients with serious and complex conditions. It is within the constraints of this emerging literature that this committee determined its final conclusions and recommendations concerning persons with serious and complex medical conditions.

3

Conclusions and Recommendations

INTRODUCTION

Throughout the course of this study, the committee has been extremely aware of the fact that the topic addressed by this report concerns one of the most critical issues confronting HCFA, health care plans and providers, and patients today. The Medicare+Choice regulations focus on the most vulnerable populations in need of medical care and other services—those with serious or complex medical conditions. Caring for these highly vulnerable populations poses a number of challenges.

In the absence of a fully developed research and clinical knowledge base, combined with the time and resource constraints of this study, the committee chose what it believes is the most prudent and thoughtful approach to its charge. Specifically, the committee has chosen to provide guidance to HCFA and health care plans to support initial steps to address the major issues confronting health care plans and their beneficiaries with serious and complex medical conditions. This guidance is supported by presentation of possible strategies that might be used to screen enrollees for the presence of serious and complex medical conditions. Health care plans are encouraged to be innovative in their initial efforts to develop case-screening methodologies. As plans develop experience with different screening modalities, information can be shared nationally. It is the committee's intent that this will lead to the identification of best practices and subsequent standardized methods for ongoing screening of beneficiaries for serious and complex conditions. The committee also recommends strategies to ensure that the care offered to persons with serious and complex conditions is responsive to the diverse, multidisciplinary needs for services to address a full spectrum of medical, social, and mental health issues. Finally, the committee feels strongly that evaluation and research efforts must occur simultaneously with the implementation of the guidance and recommendations concerning screening and care of patients with serious and complex medical conditions. As HCFA and health care plans develop the necessary expertise and resources to provide comprehensive, multidisciplinary care to patients with serious and complex conditions, this knowledge can be generalized to address the needs of patients with serious but not complex and complex but not serious medical conditions. The following conclusions and recommendations are based on consideration of these diverse issues.

Recommendation 1: The establishment of an administrative definition for serious and complex medical conditions by the Health Care Financing Administration would be premature at this time.

It is the opinion of the committee that the current state of clinical and research literature does not support development of an operational definition for serious and complex medical conditions. There are a large number of potential ways to screen and identify patients with serious and complex medical conditions, although each has its own set of limitations. Disease classification systems such as diagnosis-related groups, diagnostic cost groups, and the *International Classification of Diseases—Ninth Edition* lack the sensitivity and specificity required to effectively distinguish between patients with acute care needs and those who need more extensive treatment and service arrays. The validity of patient classifications systems (e.g., diagnosis-related groups) and functional status definitions (e.g., Karnofsky and SF-36 scales) has not yet been determined. Efforts to develop case-mix-adjusted reimbursement systems to ensure cost-effectiveness and high-quality interventions for patients with serious and complex conditions are still in the early stages or are limited to only a single disease category. Similarly, efforts to develop standardized protocols for care coordination, continuity of care, care management strategies, and service reimbursement plans have met with varying degrees of success.

Clinical research relevant to defining patient populations as having serious and complex conditions and developing the most effective care protocols to respond to patient needs is evolving rapidly, but only preliminary results are available. For example, research in correlating patient volume with patient outcomes, differentiating access to services as a function of health plan benefits, and addressing variations in quality of care has just begun to yield meaningful results about particular groups of patients. The committee anticipates that this research will continue to evolve and will provide more definitive conclusions to guide the efforts of health plans to identify patients with serious and complex medical conditions and ensure appropriate levels of treatment and care management. As the science base is strengthened, so too will be the ability of HCFA and health plans to correctly identify patients with serious and complex medical conditions who would benefit from broad strategies of care management.

Recognizing these limitations, the committee recommends that plans first focus their attentions on patient populations with conditions that are serious

AND complex. These conditions are described as persistent, substantially disabling or life threatening that require treatments and interventions across a broad scope of medical, social, and mental health services. Plans will require time to develop expertise and resources to develop methods of case finding and provision of an integrated care management approach for these patients. As such expertise is developed and resources are allocated, plans can then expand their efforts to include patients with serious but not complex conditions and those with complex but not serious conditions.

> **Recommendation 2:** The committee recommends that the Health Care Financing Administration should provide *guidance* to health plans to assist their efforts to identify patients with serious and complex medical conditions. Specifically, the committee recommends the following language be used to facilitate efforts of plans to identify their enrollees with "serious and complex conditions": "A *serious and complex* condition is one that is persistent and substantially disabling or life threatening that requires treatments and services across a variety of domains of care to ensure the best possible outcomes for each unique patient of member."

The committee recognizes the importance at this time of providing health plans with **guidance** to facilitate operationalization of their own definitions of serious and complex medical conditions. This guidance includes a description of a serious and complex medical condition as one that is persistent and substantially disabling or life threatening that requires treatments and services across a variety of domains of care. The committee reviewed a number of possible categories of conditions that might be considered serious and complex. These are discussed in Chapter 1 of this report and include, but are not limited to, life-threatening conditions, conditions that cause serious disability without necessarily being life threatening, conditions associated with severe consequences, conditions affecting multiple organ systems, conditions requiring coordination of management by multiple specialties, and conditions requiring treatments that carry a risk of serious complications.

Clinical research to identify patient populations with serious and complex medical conditions and develop the most effective care management strategies to respond to patient needs is evolving rapidly, with only preliminary results available. The current state of clinical and research literature does not adequately address all of the challenges and issues relevant to the identification and care of these patients. These issues include, but are not limited to, identification of methods and criteria that can be applied to screen enrollees for the presence of serious and complex conditions; development of strategies for proper care and management of the complex array of medical, social, and mental health problems confronting these patients; development of strategies to evaluate the effectiveness, efficacy, and efficiency of different strategies of care management; and ongoing research to ensure continuous improvements in the care of patients. Health care service research is only beginning to emerge with initial findings relevant to these issues.

The committee anticipates that this research will continue to evolve and provide more definitive conclusions to guide the efforts of health plans to identify patients with serious and complex medical conditions and help plans to provide appropriate levels of treatment and care management. The committee urges health care plans, in collaboration with federal agencies and research institutions, to support this ongoing research and facilitate a synthesis of emerging results. As the science base is strengthened, so too will be the ability of HCFA and health plans to correctly identify patients who would benefit from a broad care management strategy including those with serious but not complex or complex but not serious conditions.

Recommendation 3: The committee recommends that health plans develop a broad strategy for care management to enable patients and providers to achieve the best possible outcomes for each unique patient or member with a serious or complex medical condition.

This care management strategy should include, but not necessarily be limited to, case finding; screening and selection; problem assessment and identification of strengths; development of treatment or care plans; implementation of care plans with an emphasis on proactive interventions; and monitoring of care plan implementation and outcomes.

The treatments for individuals with serious and complex medical conditions will inevitably vary due to many factors, including characteristics of the individual patient and the patient's social situation, characteristics of individual providers, provider organizations, health plans, resources in the community, health plan benefits, and so forth. Although these factors will vary for all patients, they have less impact on preventive care (e.g., immunizations) and acute care (e.g., setting a broken arm) interventions. Successful outcomes for persons with serious and complex medical conditions will rely on a diverse mix of medical, social, functional, financial, and psychological factors, as well as on how these factors mesh with a community's health and social services resources. There is no single guideline that can prescribe the care or treatments for persons with serious and complex medical conditions.

The committee's recommendations concerning elements of the care management strategy have been derived, in part, from existing publications (Case Management Society of America, 1996; HMO Workgroup on Care Management, 1999). A brief explanation for each of the recommended steps in the care process is provided below.

Case finding refers to methods for identifying persons who may have a serious and complex medical condition. Utilization of the committee's recommended description for serious and complex conditions can facilitate efforts by health plans and providers to identify possible categories of patients for whom case finding should be conducted. Depending on the organization of a health plan and its provider group(s), case finding methods may include electronic searching of administrative databases; phone screening of new or existing members; referral by patient or family member; referral by a clinician or other professional; or notification by an emergency room, hospital, nursing home, or other provider organization.

Case screening and selection outline a process for deciding exactly which patients meet a plan's criteria for serious and complex medical conditions. These criteria should be established by each health plan with review by HCFA. Examples of selection criteria might include factors such as diagnostic codes, patient age, presence of comorbidities, severity of illness or disability, duration of a disability, and so forth. It is expected that patients meeting these criteria would benefit from coordinated care management.

The next step in the care process should involve an assessment of the patient's problems and strengths. This is a tool for gathering information about the patient's medical, social, functional, and financial status that will be used to further determine his or her need for care management and the resources available to access the necessary services.

Treatment or care planning is also recommended by the committee as an essential element of a care management strategy for patients with serious and complex medical conditions. Such planning supports the development of individualized, goal-focused care plans (based on assessment findings and drawing on evidence-based treatments when available) to provide a guide for delineating patient, provider, and plan responsibilities for accessing and coordinating needed services.

The care management strategy also demands that steps be taken to ensure the implementation of care plans. Execution of the care management plan includes strategies and tactics for providing or purchasing needed services, or for linking patients to covered services, services available in the community, or those for which the patient will have to pay. It also includes advocating for the provision of informal services by family, friends, and neighbors.

The final step of the care process is monitoring implementation and outcomes of the care management strategy. This can be based upon periodic reviews of a patient's status and treatments to determine whether goals are being achieved, whether interventions and treatments continue to be appropriate, whether there is a medical need for continued services, or whether proactive care is required to address potential or emerging new problems. This type of monitoring can also include measurements to assess the impact of care management and treatment on clinical, functional, cost, and satisfaction outcomes.

Throughout the entire care management strategy for persons with serious and complex medical conditions, three principles should be evident. First, the care management strategy should reflect a commitment to continuity and coordination of care, as described among the requirements for National Committee for Quality Assurance accreditation. This entails monitoring continuity and coordination activities, analyzing data to identify opportunities for improvement, and taking actions to bring about improvements, as indicated. Second, the care process should include multidisciplinary perspectives and treatments, as appropriate. The care of persons with serious and complex medical conditions may require the assessment and treatment expertise of primary care providers; medical and surgical specialists; nurses and nurse specialists; social workers; pharmacists; occupational, speech, and physical therapists; behavioral and mental health professionals; and community-based service providers and resources. Access to expertise from these various disciplines should be available as needed. Third, and perhaps most important, patients and their family members should be involved at every step so that the care process incorporates the patient's expectations and preferences and documents the patient's role in achieving treatment goals.

The committee's recommendations concerning the care management process for patients with serious and complex conditions assumes patient willingness to collaborate with a multidisciplinary team of providers in the development and implementation of that plan. In those instances where a patient or family member declines such participation, appropriate documentation should be entered into the patient record. The presence of such documentation should be considered by HCFA as evidence that a good faith effort has been made by the plan to involve the patient and family in the development of the case management plan.

Recommendation 4: The committee recommends that health plans design and implement strategies for routine screening and selection to identify those beneficiaries with serious and complex medical conditions. These strategies should be consistent with the guidance outlined in Recommendation 2 to determine which patients meet a plan's threshold for serious and complex medical conditions and would benefit from a coordinated care management strategy.

The committee recommends that health plans identify specific categories of patients or health conditions for which screening for the presence of serious and complex conditions should occur on a routine basis. Examples of such categories are provided in Chapter 1. The committee is of the opinion that screening a health care plan's entire population of enrollees is not a feasible, cost-effective, or efficient method of identifying subpopulations with serious and complex medical conditions. The committee feels strongly, however, that early efforts to develop case-screening methodologies should not be prescriptive; rather, innovation should be encouraged. Documentation of locally derived methods by plans will result in extensive nationwide experience that can be assessed and can lead to the identification of best practices and subsequent standardized methods for ongoing routine screening of patient populations.

The appropriate application of resources by a health plan to patients with serious and complex medical conditions requires the identification of those individuals whose health outcomes would benefit by such designation. For the purposes of this report, the committee has not included patients suffering from acute conditions that might require coordinated delivery of sophisticated medical services to treat complications of acute decompensation. On the other hand, many patients who have endured prolonged hospitalization for an acute medical condition may subsequently need coordinated long-term care to maximize their rehabilitation potential; to treat persistent sequelae of the disease processes that resulted from the acute, severe illness; and to ensure that they receive proactive care to prevent further exacerbation of the illness or disability.

Conceptually, various methodologies could be applied to administrative databases that could produce relevant lists of patients with serious and complex medical conditions who would be likely to benefit from written care management plans. High-cost patients, for example, might merit designation as having serious and complex conditions. Some of these individuals, however, may have undergone a single event such as bypass surgery that is self-limited and not appropriate for such designation. In contrast, others will have conditions, such as organ transplants, disabling traumatic injury, and HIV/AIDS, that clearly require ongoing medical attention and resources to sustain or improve their health status. Aside from costs, certain diagnostic entities could be identified for designation as serious and complex medical conditions. Examples of such entities could include progressive, degenerative disorders, active collagen vascular disease, and metastatic cancers. The committee does not believe it is feasible at this time to create an all-encompassing list of diagnoses appropriate for designation as serious and complex conditions. Indeed, within any diagnostic label, there exists a continuum of disease and disability that requires varying degrees of medical and other health-related support.

Beneficiary survey tools could supplement the use of administrative data sets to identify appropriate patients. Questionnaires that quantify functional status could assist plans in capturing individuals who need special attention in the outpatient setting to improve or sustain functional capacity or physiological stability. Similarly, home health agencies or medical professionals could identify frail elderly patients who require care management to sustain homeostasis. These agents could refer patients' names to health plans for development of a formal management program for serious and complex medical conditions. Such patients could include those of advanced age (over 85) with several comorbid medical conditions such as congestive heart failure, chronic renal failure, and diabetes. These persistent conditions in concert with reduced cognitive functioning or physical capacity to sustain daily living activities produce a constellation of physiological deficits that require supportive health care services for the patient to maintain independent living in a community setting.

There are several reasons why it is essential to the care of persons with serious and complex medical conditions that screening and selection of a plan's designated patient categories or conditions occur on a routine basis. First, periodic screening allows the multidisciplinary care team to adjust the care management approach as patient needs change over time. Second, routine screening is necessary to identify new patients with serious and complex medical conditions. Third, it ensures that persons who are no longer considered to have a serious and complex condition will be identified and services adjusted accordingly, which could result in a cost benefit.

The committee believes that over time, the health care system will identify reliable, accurate screening techniques for populations of patients with serious and complex medical conditions. In many cases, timely identification will permit appropriate treatment at the level of the primary care provider. Nevertheless, even with robust methodologies in place, there will be patients and families who believe that they require additional resources or attention to adequately manage a persistent health condition. In instances in which a treatment plan is not mutually agreeable, individuals should be able to appeal to the medical director of the provider group or health plan. The review process should be timely and should allow for both internal and independent external review.

> **Recommendation 5:** The committee recommends that health care plans develop a care management strategy that integrates the participation of all those involved in the care of the patient, including primary care physicians; medical and surgical specialists; nurses and nurse specialists; behavioral and mental health specialists; physical, occupational, and speech therapists; social workers; allied health professionals; and community-based service providers.

The development of a collaborative care management strategy involving all those who participate in providing care to the individual patient is critical to the treatment of patients with serious and complex conditions. The treatment plan serves several important functions within the care management strategy. First, it provides a road map and a guide to indicate direction of and demarcate landmarks in care management, making it easier to ensure that all providers involved in the patient's care share the same goals, and that these goals are accessible to the patient and the patient's family. Second, it provides a way to measure progress and the achievement of care goals, and it serves as a powerful communication and coordination tool among the participants involved in the care of the patient, avoiding overlapping or redundant efforts as well as gaps and inattention to components of care assumed to be the responsibility of others on the care team. Third, a treatment plan offers an opportunity to delineate which provider is taking responsibility for specific aspects of care.

Although there is currently no evidence to support the identification of a single format or model as superior to all others, the committee feels confident in recommending certain key components that should be part of any treatment plan for patients with serious and complex medical conditions. Specifically, the plan should involve the collaborative participation of all those taking part in the care of the patient, including primary care physicians; medical and surgical specialists; nurses and nurse specialists; physical, occupational, and speech therapists; rehabilitation specialists; behavioral and mental health specialists; social workers; allied health professionals; and community-based service providers and resources.

The perspectives, health beliefs, and values of the patient and the patient's family should be taken into consideration, and the care management plan should be constructed in a culturally appropriate manner. Elements of the care management plan should be appropriate both for the age or life phase of each patient as well as the stage or severity of the health condition. This will ensure selection of treatment options that are responsive to the unique needs of patients of different age groups and with conditions of varying severity. The patient should be involved in the development of the plan and should have access to the plan.

The plan should be linked to relevant clinical practice guidelines and should reflect the process of adapting population-based clinical practice guidelines to the unique care and service needs of the individual. The treatment plan should cross areas of expertise and should address the need for coordination of care across the continuum of care delivery settings. The plan should be longitudinal, with accommodations for proactive interventions to prevent potential problems from arising, and it should also enable longitudinal assessment of outcomes. The treatment plan should be a living document that is periodically reviewed, updated, and tested for continuing relevance to the patient's circumstances (e.g., the life phase) and clinical condition (e.g., the disease stage).

Recommendation 6: The committee recommends that health care plans have programs in place to monitor care management plans for both process and outcomes for patients with serious and complex conditions at the level of population, patient, provider, and best practices of care.

The Health Care Financing Administration should establish a formal mechanism to evaluate a Medicare+Choice provider organization's program to monitor the outcomes of care for patients with serious and complex medical conditions. The committee recognizes that the monitoring and evaluation programs will vary between health plans but recommends that all programs include population-based monitoring of the outcomes of care for patients with serious or complex conditions, as well as individual case monitoring, assessment of provider interventions, and evaluation of best practices of care.

Assessment of population-based measures may include, but not be limited to, review of plan-wide policies and procedures; application of working definitions of serious and complex conditions; adoption of evidence-based clinical guidelines; review of health outcomes survey, patient satisfaction and complaint data; and review of clinical outcomes data for patients with serious or complex medical conditions. Individual case monitoring may include, but not be limited to, analysis of complaint data, patient satisfaction, internal and external appeals of the care plan, and overturned denials. Evaluation and monitoring at the level of providers will include efforts to assess clinical quality of care, timeliness of care, and effectiveness of specific interventions. Best practices of care will be identified by data that describe clinical, functional, and patient satisfaction outcomes.

Recommendation 7: The committee recommends that the Health Care Financing Administration collaborate with federal, private, and voluntary agencies, organizations, and consumers to establish an ongoing process to address policy issues to ensure continuous improvements in the care of populations with serious and complex medical conditions.

Access to providers with the appropriate training and expertise is important, but other issues must be addressed to ensure that beneficiaries with serious and complex conditions achieve the best possible outcomes. The committee recognizes that a number of these issues supersede activities that can be accomplished at the level of individual health plans. Issues that must be addressed include, but are not limited to, the following:

• *Payment.* The current Medicare capitated payment mechanisms for health plans are not risk adjusted and are derived from experience in the fee-for-service sector. These payment mechanisms may not provide adequate compensation to some health plans. Furthermore, health plans use a variety of methods to compensate individual providers and hospitals. Greater attention should be focused on the improved alignment of financial incentives at all levels to ensure appropriate payment for serious and complex cases through adequate funding and risk-adjusted payment systems.

• *Benefits.* Improving the care of persons with serious and complex medical conditions can be supported by ensuring that Medicare beneficiaries can choose among different health plans. When beneficiaries have multiple affordable options, they can select based upon their own evaluations of quality. Where benefits are provided through multiple payment programs (i.e., Medicare and Medicaid dual eligibles), coordination of benefit packages and eligibility requirements is critical. The movement of patients with serious and complex conditions into managed care holds the promise of greater health for these patients and therefore reduced expenditures for Medicaid programs due to reduced nursing home use. Prescription coverage for these patients would result in a direct reduction in state Medicaid prescription coverage expenses. Medicare requirements for management of patients with serious and complex conditions may also serve as the future basis for Medicaid managed care contracts.

• *Medicaid and Medicare Fee-for-Service Programs.* The committee was unable to address the third point of its charge with any degree of thoroughness. This is primarily due to the fact that the committee lacked sufficient information and time to conduct informed deliberations about the implications of alternative definitions for serious and complex medical conditions for Medicaid and commercial programs, especially when applied to Medicare beneficiaries who are dual eligible. The committee strongly recommends that HCFA, in collaboration with Medicare and Medicaid provider plans, establish this as a research priority. Resources and expertise should be allocated to conduct a study to define the relevant issues and generate possible approaches to address this question.

In the meantime, the committee suggests that the basic guidance provided in this report concerning the description of serious and complex medical conditions and recommendations concerning strategies for care management for this patient population should be extended to include Medicaid beneficiaries and those that are dual eligible. In addition, this guidance should apply to patients enrolled in fee-for-service Medicare programs. This should be a priority area for collaborative research on policy issues to ensure continuous improvements in the care of populations with serious and complex medical conditions covered by Medicaid and fee-for-service Medicare plans.

- *Consumer Education and Participation.* Many patients, especially those with persistent and disabling conditions, are ready and able to become more active participants in the care delivery process. Attempts should be made to increase patient participation in clinical decision-making and caregiving processes consistent with improving clinical outcomes and satisfaction.

- *Professional Training.* To serve persons with serious and complex medical conditions, an aggressive strategy must be developed to educate and train health professionals to provide appropriate care for this population. There is currently a great undersupply of persons trained in care management processes, multidisciplinary team care, geriatrics, patient education and self-management, and cultural competence.

- *Information Technology.* More sophisticated information technology is required to provide high-quality, coordinated care to those with complex or serious medical conditions. More sophisticated information systems are needed to support efforts to monitor, analyze, and improve patient care. Continued development of electronic medical records will be an important factor in ensuring that all health care organizations and providers involved in the care of a patient have timely access to complete information on the patient's clinical conditions, diagnostic and therapeutic test results, and services received. Confidentiality protections must be respected throughout the process of technology development.

- *Regulatory Framework.* Developing a regulatory approach for the Medicare+Choice program that affords adequate protections for beneficiaries with serious and complex medical conditions while encouraging innovation in a rapidly changing health care environment will be an ongoing challenge. Periodic evaluation and modification will be essential.

- *Applied Research.* Research is needed to further inform the policy process and to identify best practices in the care of patients with serious and complex conditions. Attention should be focused on the following areas: effects of benefits coverage and payment methods on care delivery; determination and dissemination of best practices in the identification of patients with serious and complex conditions; efficacy, effectiveness, and efficiency of multidisciplinary teams; use of information technology to support care coordination and delivery; and development of innovative methods of designing, implementing, and coordinating medical, social, and other services.

These and related issues will require HCFA to actively collaborate with all types of payors, health care plans, providers, research organizations, and consumer and disability groups to develop strategies and solutions that will maximize the quality of health care and other services for patients with serious and complex medical conditions.

CONCLUSIONS

The needs of patients with serious and complex medical conditions far exceed the boundaries of a single issue such as access to specialists for care. For health care delivery systems to provide high-quality, effective care for these patients, the systems must be responsive to a diverse array of clinical, social, mental, and functional health issues. The development of a health care delivery system that will provide quality and effective care for these patient populations must be responsive to a diverse group of clinical, social, mental, and functional health issues. The health care delivery system must also be capable of working effectively with other community and social support systems.

The questions raised by HCFA concerning implementation and regulations for the Medicare+Choice program apply broadly to include all health care delivery and payment systems, including fee-for-service care. This study is one of the first to address these complex and extremely important topics. Thus, the committee urges HCFA, health care plans, and consumer groups to view this report, and especially its conclusions and recommendations, as first steps in the effort to address the unique and complicated needs of persons with serious and complex medical conditions and to ensure that they receive the most cost-effective and best-quality care possible. The work of this committee is intended to support and provide direction for future work to be conducted by HCFA, in collaboration with all types of health care plans and consumer organizations, to design innovative strategies to ensure adequate reimbursement, access to broad care management, and the highest possible quality of treatment services required by patients with serious and complex medical conditions.

References

Aday LA. Health status of vulnerable populations. *Annual Review of Public Health* 15:487–509, 1994.

Aday LA, Andersen R. Equity of access to medical care: A conceptual and empirical overview. *Medical Care* 19(Suppl 12):4–27, 1981.

Aday LA, Begley CE, Lairson DR, et al. *Evaluating the Medical Care System: Effectiveness, Efficiency, and Equity.* Ann Arbor, MI: Health Administration Press, 1993a.

Aday LA, Lee ES, Spears B, et al. Health insurance and utilization of medical care for children with special health care needs. *Medical Care* 31(11):1013–1026, 1993b.

American Medical Association. *International Classification of Diseases* (9th Revision—Clinical Modification). Chicago: American Medical Association, 1999.

American Psychiatric Association. *Diagnostic and Statistical Manual of Mental Disorders* (Fourth Edition). Washington, DC: American Psychiatric Association, 1994.

Ash A, Proell F, Grunenberg L, et al. Adjusting Medicare capitation payments using prior hospitalization data. *Health Care Financing Review* Summer:17–30, 1989.

Banta D, Bos M. The relation between quantity and quality with coronary artery bypass graft (CABG) surgery. *Health Policy* 18:1–10, 1991.

Banta HD, Engel GL, and Schersten T. Volume and outcome of organ transplantation. International Journal of Technology *Assessment in Health Care* 8(3):490–505, 1991.

Bennett CL, Adams J, Bennett RL, et al. The learning curve for AIDS-related *Pneumocystis carinii* pneumonia: Experience from 3,981 cases in Veterans Affairs hospitals, 1987–1991. *Journal of Acquired Immune Deficiency Syndromes and Human Retrovirology* 8:373–378, 1995.

Bennett CL, Garfinkle JB, Greenfield S, et al. The relation between hospital experience and in-hospital mortality for patients with AIDS-related PCP. *Journal of the American Medical Association* 261:2975–2979, 1989.

Bernard AM, Shapiro LR, McMahon LF. The influence of attending physician subspecialization on hospital length of stay. *Medical Care* 28(2):170–174, 1990.

Bindman AB, Grumbach K, Osmond D, et al. Primary care and receipt of preventive services. *Journal of General Internal Medicine* 11:269–276, 1996.

Blazer DG, Landerman LR, Fillenbaum G, Horner R. Health services access and use among older adults in North Carolina urban versus rural residents. *American Journal of Public Health* 85:1384–1390, 1995.

Bradbury RC, Stearns FE, Steen PM. Inter-hospital variations in admission severity-adjusted hospital mortality and morbidity. *Health Services Research* 26(4):407–424, 1991.

Brook RH, Kamberg CJ, Lohr KN, Goldberg GA, Keeler, EB, Newhouse JP. Quality of ambulatory care: Epidemiology and comparison by insurance status and income. *Medical Care* 28:392–433, 1990.

Bunker JP. Surgical manpower. A comparison of operations and surgeons in the United States and in England and Wales. *New England Journal of Medicine* 282(3):135–144, 1970.

Case Management Society of America. *Standards of Practice for Case Management.* Little Rock, AR: Case Management Society of America, 1996.

Cherkin DC, Rosenblatt RA, Hart LG, et al. The use of medical resources by residency-trained family physicians and general internists. *Medical Care* 25(6):455–469, 1987.

Choti MA, Bowman, HM, Pitt, HA, et al. Should hepatic resections be performed at high-volume referral centers? *Journal of Gastrointestinal Surgery* 2:11–20, 1998.

DesHarnais SI. Enrollment in and disenrollment from health maintenance organizations by Medicaid recipients. *Health Care Financing Review* 6:39–50, 1985.

Dowd B, Christianson J, Feldman R, et al. Issues regarding health plan payments under Medicare and recommendations for reform. *Milbank Quarterly* 70:423–453, 1992.

Eisenberg JM. *Doctors' Decisions and the Cost of Medical Care: The Reasons for Doctors' Practice Patterns and Ways to Change Them.* Ann Arbor, MI: Health Administration Press, 1986.

Ellis RP, Pope GC, Iezzoni L, et al. Diagnosis-based risk adjustment for Medicare capitation payments. *Health Care Financing Review* 17:101–128, 1996.

Elnicki DM, Morris DK, Shockcor WT. Patient-perceived barriers to preventive health care among indigent, rural Appalachian patients. *Archives of Internal Medicine* 155:421–424, 1995.

Employee Benefits Research Institute. *EBRI Databook on Employee Benefits.* Washington, DC: Employee Benefits Research Institute, 1997.

Erlich P. Informal support networks meet health needs of rural elderly. *Journal of Gerontological Social Work* 9:85, 1985.

Espehaug B, Havelin LI, Engesaeter LB, et al. The effect of hospital-type and operating volume on the survival of hip replacements. *Acta Orthopaedica Scandinavia* 70(1):12–18, 1999.

Fama T, Fox P, White LA. Do HMOs care for the chronically ill? *Health Affairs* 14:234–243, 1995.

Farley DE, Ozminkowski RJ. Volume–outcome relationships and in hospital mortality: The effect of changes in volume over time. *Medical Care* 30(1):77–94, 1992.

Feinglass J, Martin GJ, Sen A. The financial effect of physician practice style on hospital resource use. *Health Services Research* 26(2):183–205, 1991.

Fine MJ, Orloff JJ, Arisumi D, et al. Prognosis of patients hospitalized with community-acquired pneumonia. *American Journal of Medicine* 88(5N):1N–8N, 1990.

Folland S, Stano M. Sources of small area variations in the use of medical care. *Journal of Health Economics* 8(1):85–107, 1989.

Folland S, Stano M. Small area variations: A critical review of propositions, methods, and evidence. *Medical Care Review* 47(4):419–465, 1990.

Forrest CB, Starfield B. Entry into primary care and continuity: The effects of access. *American Journal of Public Health* 88(9):1330–1336, 1998.
Fox HB, Newacheck PW. Private health insurance of chronically ill children. *Pediatrics* 85(1):50–57, 1990.
Franks P, Dickinson JC. Comparisons of family physicians and internists: Process and outcome in adult patients at a community hospital. *Medical Care* 24(10):941–948, 1986.
Frenzen PD. The increasing supply of physicians in U.S. urban and rural areas, 1975 to 1988. *American Journal of Public Health* 81:1141–1147, 1991.
Freund D, Hurley R. Medicaid managed care. Contribution to issues of health reform. *Annual Review of Public Health* 16:473–495, 1995.
Freund D, Lewit E. Managed care for children and pregnant women. Promises and pitfalls. *The Future of Children* 3:2–122, 1993.
Garber AM, Fuchs VR, Silverman JF. Case mix, costs, and outcomes: Differences between faculty and community services in a university hospital. *New England Journal of Medicine* 310(19):1231–1237, 1984.
Garg ML, Mulligan JL, Gliebe WA, et al. Physician specialty, quality and cost of inpatient care. *Social Science and Medicine* 13C:187–190, 1979.
Gemson DH, Elinson J. Prevention in primary care: Variability in physician practice patterns in New York City. *American Journal of Preventive Medicine* 2:226–234, 1986.
Geraci JM, Rosen AK, Ash AS, et al. Predicting the occurrence of adverse events after coronary artery bypass surgery. *Annals of Internal Medicine* 118(1):18–24, 1993.
Gibbons J, Camp H, Kaiser M. Patterns of long-term-care services for the rural elderly: A community approach. *Human Services in the Rural Environment* 14:6, 1991.
Gittelsohn A, Powe NR. Small area variations in health care delivery in Maryland. *Health Services Research* 30(2):295–317, 1995.
Gonnella JS, Louis, DZ, Zeleznik C, et al. The problem of late hospitalization: A quality and cost issue. *Academic Medicine* 65(5):314–319, 1990.
Greenfield S, Nelson EC, Zuboff M, et al. Variation in resource utilization among medical specialties and systems of care: Results from the Medical Outcomes Study. *Journal of the American Medical Association* 267(12):1624–1630, 1992.
Greenwald HP, Peterson ML, Garrison LP, et al. Inter-specialty variation in office-based care. *Medical Care* 22(1):14–29, 1984.
Hannan EL. The relation between volume and outcome in health care. *New England Journal of Medicine* 340:1677–1679, 1991.
Hannan EL, Kilburn H, Bernard H, et al. Coronary artery bypass surgery: The relationship between in-hospital mortality rate and surgical volume after controlling for clinical risk factors. *Medical Care* 29(11):1094–1107, 1991.
Hannan EL, Siu AL, Kumar D, et al. The decline in coronary artery bypass graft surgery mortality in New York State: The role of surgeon volume. *Journal of the American Medical Association* 273:209–213, 1995.
Hannan EL, Kilburn H, O'Donnell JF, et al. A longitudinal analysis of the relationship between in-hospital mortality in New York State and the volume of abdominal aortic aneurysm surgeries performed. *Health Services Research* 27(4):517–542, 1997a.
Hannan EL, Kilburn H, Racz M, et al. Improving the outcomes of coronary artery bypass surgery in New York State. *Journal of the American Medical Association* 271:761–766, 1994.
Hannan EL, Racz M, Kavey RE, et al. Pediatric cardiac surgery: The effect of hospital and surgeon volume on in-hospital mortality. *Pediatrics* 101(6):963–969, 1998.

Hannan EL, Racz M, Ryan TJ, et al. Coronary angioplasty volume–outcome relationships for hospitals and cardiologists. *Journal of the American Medical Association* 279: 892–899, 1997b.

Hartley RM, Charlton JR, Harris CM, et al. Patterns of physicians' use of medical resources in ambulatory settings. *American Journal of Public Health* 77(5):565–567, 1987.

Hawkes J. 1st consumer guide to hospitals compares costs, results in region. *Intelligence Journal* 1:1–6, 1989.

Hill JW, Brown RS. *Biased Selection in the TEFRA HMO/CMP Program.* Princeton, NJ: Mathematica Policy Research, 1990.

Hillner BE, Smith TJ. The quality of cancer care: Does the literature support the rhetoric? In Institute of Medicine, *Ensuring Quality Cancer Care.* Washington, DC: National Academy Press, 1999.

HMO Workgroup on Care Management. *Identifying High-Risk Medicare HMO Members and Geriatric Case Management: Challenges and Potential Solutions in Managed Care Organizations.* Washington, DC: American Association of Health Plans, 1999.

Hofer TP, Katz SJ. Healthy behaviors among women in the United States and Ontario: The effect of use on preventive care. *American Journal of Public Health* 86:1755–1759, 1996.

Holahan J, Zuckerman S, Evans A, et al. Medicaid managed care in thirteen states. *Health Affairs* 17(3):43–63, 1998.

Horn SD, Horn RA, Moses H. Profiles of physician practice and patient severity of illness. *American Journal of Public Health* 76(5):532–535, 1986.

Horn SD, Sharkey PD, Buckle JM, et al. The relationship between severity of illness and hospital length of stay and mortality. *Medical Care* 29(4):305–317, 1991.

Hughes RG, Garnick DW, Luft HS, et al. Hospital volume and patient outcomes: The case of hip fracture patients. *Medical Care* 26:1057–1067, 1988.

Hughes RG, Hunt SS, Luft HS. Effects of surgeon volume and hospital volume on quality of care in hospitals. *Medical Care* 25(6):489–503, 1987.

Hurtado AV, Greenlick MR. A disease classification system for analysis of medical care utilization, with a note on symptom classification. *Health Services Research* 6:235–250, 1971.

Iezzoni LI, Ash AS, Cobb JL, et al. Admission MedisGroups score and the cost of hospitalizations. *Medical Care* 26(11):1069–1080. 1988.

Iezzoni LI, Ash AS, Coffman G, et al. Admission and mid-stay MedisGroups scores as predictors of death within 30 days of hospital admission. *American Journal of Public Health* 81(1):74–78, 1991.

Iezzoni LI, Daley J, Heeren T, et al. Using administrative data to screen hospitals for high complication rates. *Inquiry* 31:40–55, 1994a.

Iezzoni LI, Foley SM, Heeren T, et al. A method for screening the quality of hospital care using administrative data: Preliminary validation results. *Quality Review Bulletin* 18: 361–371, 1992.

Iezzoni LI, Heeren T, Foley SM, et al. Chronic conditions and risk of in-hospital death. *Health Services Research* 29(4):435–460, 1994b.

Imperiale TF, Siegal AP, Crede WB, et al. Pre-admission screening of Medicare patients. The clinical impact of reimbursement disapproval. *Journal of the American Medical Association* 259(23):3418–3421, 1988.

Institute of Medicine. *Controlling Costs and Changing Patient Care? The Role of Utilization Management.* Washington, DC: National Academy Press, 1989.

Institute of Medicine. *Medicare. A Strategy for Quality Assurance* (Volume 1). Washington, DC: National Academy Press, 1990.
Institute of Medicine. *Developing an Information Infrastructure for the Medicare+ Choice Program. Summary of a Workshop.* Washington, DC: National Academy Press, 1999.
Institute of Medicine. *Ensuring Quality Cancer Care.* Washington, DC: National Academy Press, 1999.
Institute of Medicine, National Roundtable on Health Care Quality. *Measuring the Quality of Health Care.* Washington, DC: National Academy Press, 1999.
Ireys HT, Grason HA, Guyer B. Assuring quality of care for children with special needs in managed care organizations: Roles for pediatricians. *Pediatrics* 98(2):178–185, 1996.
Jollis JG, Peterson ED, DeLong ER, et al. The relation between the volume of coronary angioplasty procedures at hospitals treating Medicare beneficiaries and short-term mortality. *New England Journal of Medicine* 331(24):1625–1629, 1994.
Kaiser Family Foundation and the Agency for Health Care Policy and Research. *Americans as Health Care Consumers: The Role of Quality Information.* Princeton, NJ: Princeton Survey Research Associates, 1996.
Kantonen I, Lepantalo M, Salenius J-P, et al. Influence of surgical experience on the results of carotid surgery. *Journal of Vascular and Endovascular Surgery* 15:155–160, 1998.
Kaplan RM, Anderson JP, Mathews WC, et al. The Quality of Well-Being Scale: Applications in AIDS, cystic fibrosis, and arthritis. *Medical Care* 27:S27–S43, 1989.
Karnofsky DA, Burchenal JH. The clinical evaluation of chemotherapeutic agents. In McLeod CM (Ed.), *Evaluation of Chemotherapeutic Agents.* New York: Columbia University Press, 1949.
Katz S, Ford AB, Moskowitz RW. The index of ADL: A standardized measure of biological and social function. *Journal of the American Medical Association* 185:914–919, 1963.
Kellie SE, Kelly JT. Medicare peer review organizations pre-procedure review criteria. An analysis of criteria for three procedures. *Journal of the American Medical Association* 265(10):1265–1270, 1991.
Knaus WA, Draper EA, Wagner P, et al. An evaluation of outcome from intensive care in major medical centers. *Annals of Internal Medicine* 104(3):410–418, 1986.
Knaus WA, Wagner DP, Zimmerman JE, et al. Variations in mortality and length of stay in intensive care units. *Annals of Internal Medicine* 118(10):753–761, 1993.
Kravitz RL, Greenfield S, Rogers W, et al. Differences in the mix of patients among medical specialties and systems of care. Results from the Medical Outcomes Study. *Journal of the American Medical Association* 267(12):1617–1623, 1992.
Lambrew JM, DeFriese GH, Carey TS, et al. The effects of having a regular doctor on access to primary care. *Medical Care* 134:138, 1996.
Lamers LM. Risk-adjusted capitation based on the diagnostic cost group model: An empirical evaluation with health survey information. *Health Services Research* 33: 1727–1744, 1999.
Lave JR, Traven ND, Ives DG, et al. Participation in health promotion programs by the rural elderly. *American Journal of Preventive Medicine* 11:46–53, 1995.
Lavernia CJ, Guzman JF. Relationship of surgical volume to short-term mortality, morbidity, and hospital charges in arthroplasty. *Journal of Arthroplasty* 10(2):133–140, 1995.

Lawton MP, Brody EM. Assessment of older people: Self-maintaining and instrumental activities of daily living. *Gerontologist* 9:179–186, 1969.

Lillie-Blanton M, Lyons B. Managed care and low-income populations: Recent state experiences. *Health Affairs* 17(3):238–247, 1998.

Lillie-Blanton M, Martinez RM, Taylor AK, et al. Latina and African-American women: Continuing disparities in health. *International Journal of Health Services* 23(3):555–584, 1993.

Lillie-Blanton M, Parsons PE, Gayle H, et al. Racial differences in health: Not just black and white, but shades of gray. *Annual Review of Public Health* 17:411–448, 1996.

Linn LS, Yager J, Leake BD, et al. Differences in the numbers and costs of tests ordered by internists, family physicians, and psychiatrists. *Inquiry* 21:266–275, 1984.

Lubitz JD, Riley GF. Trends in Medicare payments in the last year of life. *New England Journal of Medicine* 328(15):1092–1096, 1993.

Luft HS. The relation between surgical volume and mortality: An exploration of causal factors and alternative models. *Medical Care* 18(9):940–959, 1980.

Luft HS, Miller RH. Patient selection in a competitive health care system. *Health Affairs* 7:97–119, 1988.

Maguire AM, Powe NR, Starfield B, et al. "Carving out" conditions from global capitation rates: Protecting high-cost patients, physicians, and health plans in a managed care environment. *American Journal of Managed Care* 4(6):797–806, 1998.

McDowell I, Newell C. *Measuring Health. A Guide to Rating Scales and Questionnaires.* New York: Oxford University Press, 1996.

McPherson K, Wennberg JE, Hovind OB, et al. Small-area variations in the use of common surgical procedures: An international comparison of New England, England, and Norway. *New England Journal of Medicine* 307(21):1310–1314, 1992.

Miller RH, Luft HS. Does managed care lead to better or worse quality of care? *Health Affairs* 6(5):7–25, 1997.

Moy E, Hogan C. Access to needed follow-up services: Variations among different Medicare populations. *Archives of Internal Medicine* 153:1815–1823, 1993.

Naessens JM, Leibson CL, Krishan I, et al. Contribution of a measure of disease complexity (COMPLEX) to prediction of outcome and charges among hospitalized patients. *Mayo Clinic Proceedings* 67(12):1140–1149, 1992.

National Hospice Organization. *Medical Guidelines for Determining Prognosis in Selected Non-Cancer Diseases* (Second Edition). Arlington, VA: National Hospice Organization, 1996.

Nelson L, Brown R, Gold M, et al. Access to care in Medicare HMOs, 1996. *Health Affairs* 148–156, 1997.

Newacheck PW, Stein REK, Walker DK, et al. Monitoring and evaluating managed care for children with chronic illness and disabilities. *Pediatrics* 98(5):952–958, 1996.

Newhouse J. Patients at risk: Health reform and risk adjustment. *Health Affairs* 13(1):132–146, 1994.

Norton EC, Garfinkel SA, McQuay LJ, et al. The effect of hospital volume on the inhospital complication rate in knee replacement patients. *Health Services Research* 33(5):1191–1210, 1998.

Oleske DM, Branca ML, Schmidt JB, et al. A comparison of capitated and fee-for-service Medicaid reimbursement methods on pregnancy outcomes. *Health Services Research* 33(1):55–73, 1998.

Phibbs CS, Bronstein JM, Buxton E, et al. The effects of patient volume and level of care at the hospital of birth on neonatal mortality. *Journal of the American Medical Association* 276(13):1054–1059, 1996.

Phillips KA, Luft HS, Ritchie JL. The association of hospital volumes of percutaneous transluminal coronary angioplasty with adverse outcomes, length of stay, and charges in California. *Medical Care* 33(5):502–514, 1995.

Powe NR, Weiner JP, Starfield B, et al. Systemwide provider performance in a Medicaid program. Profiling the care of patients with chronic illnesses. *Medical Care* 34(8): 798–810, 1996.

President's Advisory Commission on Consumer Protection and Quality in the Health Care Industry. *Consumers' Bill of Rights and Responsibilities.* Washington, DC: U.S. Government Printing Office, 1998a.

President's Advisory Commission on Consumer Protection and Quality in the Health Care Industry. *Quality First: Better Health Care for All Americans.* Washington, DC: U.S. Government Printing Office, 1998b.

Riley G, Lubitz J. Outcomes of surgery among the Medicare aged: Surgical volume and mortality. *Health Care Financing Review* 7(1):37–47, 1985.

Riley G, Lubitz J. Outcomes of surgery in the Medicare aged population: Rehospitalization after surgery. *Health Care Financing Review* 8(1):23–34, 1986.

Riley G, Lubitz J. Longitudinal patterns of Medicare use by cause of death. *Health Care Financing Review* 11(2):1–12, 1989.

Riley GF, Feuer EJ, Lubitz JD. Disenrollment of Medicare cancer patients from health maintenance organizations. *Medical Care* 34(8):826–836, 1996.

Riley G, Lubitz J, Gornick M, et al. Medicare beneficiaries: Adverse outcomes after hospitalization for eight procedures. *Medical Care* 31(10):921–949, 1993.

Riley G, Lubitz J, Prihoda R, et al. Changes in distribution of Medicare expenditures among aged enrollees, 1969–82. *Health Care Financing Review* 7(3):53–63, 1986.

Riley G, Lubitz J, Prihoda R, et al. The use and costs of Medicare services by cause of death. *Inquiry* 24(3):233–244, 1987.

Riley G, Lubitz J, Rabey E. Enrollee health status under Medicare risk contracts. An analysis of mortality rates. *Health Services Research* 26:137–163, 1991.

Riley GF, Potosky AI, Lubitz JD, et al. Stage of cancer at diagnosis for Medicare HMO and fee-for-service enrollees. *American Journal of Public Health* 84(10):1598–1604, 1994.

Riley GF, Potosky AI, Lubitz JD, et al. Medicare payments from diagnosis to death for elderly cancer patients by stage at diagnosis. *Medical Care* 33(8):828–841, 1995.

Rogers CC. *Health Status and Use of Health Care Services by the Older Population: A Residential Comparison.* Washington, DC: U.S. Department of Agriculture, 1993.

Roos NP, Flowerdew G, Wajda A, et al. Variations in physicians' hospitalization practices: A population-based study in Manitoba, Canada. *American Journal of Public Health* 76(1):45–51, 1986.

Rosenfeld K, Luft HS, Garnick WE, et al. Changes in patient characteristics and surgical outcomes for coronary artery bypass surgery. *American Journal of Public Health* 77(4):498–500, 1987.

Rossiter L, Wan T, Langwell, K, et al. *An Analysis of Patient Satisfaction for Enrollees and Disenrollees in Medicare Risk-Based Plans.* Richmond, VA: Medical College of Virginia, 1988.

Rowland D, Lyons B. Triple jeopardy: Rural, poor, and uninsured. *Health Services Research* 23(6):975–1004, 1989.

Saag KG, Doebbeling BN, Rohrer JE, et al. Variation in tertiary prevention and health service utilizations among the elderly. *Medical Care* 36(7):965–976, 1998.

Sandrick KM. Blue Cross and Blue Shield of Michigan's efforts to change practice patterns. *Quarterly Review Bulletin* 10(11):349–352, 1984.

Schlesinger M, Mechanic D. Challenges for managed competition from chronic illness. *Health Affairs* 12(Suppl):123–137, 1993.

Shwartz M, Iezzoni LI, Ash AS, et al. Do severity measures explain differences in length of hospital stay? The case of hip fracture. *Health Services Research* 31(4):365–385, 1996.

Silber JH, Williams SV, Krakauer H, et al. Hospital and patient characteristics associated with death after surgery. A Study of adverse occurrence and failure to rescue. *Medical Care* 30:615–629, 1992.

Sollanno JA, Gelijns AC, Moskowitz AJ, et al. Volume–outcome relationships in cardiovascular operations: New York State, 1990–1995. *Journal of Thoracic and Cardiovascular Surgery* 117(3):419–430, 1999.

Stafford RS, Saglam D, Causino N, et al. Trends in adult visits to primary care physicians in the United States. *Archives of Family Medicine* 8(1):26–32, 1999.

Stano M, Folland S. Variations in the use of physician services by Medicare beneficiaries. *Health Care Financing Review* 9(3):51–58, 1988.

Starfield B. Effects of poverty on health status. Bulletin of the New York Academy of Medicine 68(1):17–24, 1992.

Starfield B, Cassady C, Nanda J, et al. Consumer experiences and provider perceptions of the quality of primary care: Implications for managed care. *Journal of Family Practitioners* 46(3):216–226, 1998.

Starfield B, Powe NR, Weiner JR, et al. Costs vs quality in different types of primary care settings. *Journal of the American Medical Association* 272(24):1903–1908, 1994.

Starfield B, Shapiro S, Weiss J, et al. Race, family income, and low birth weight. American *Journal of Epidemiology* 134(10):1167–1174, 1991.

Stone VE, Seage GR, Hertz T, et al. The relation between hospital experience and mortality for patients with AIDS. *Journal of the American Medical Association.* 268(19):2655–2661, 1992.

Sullivan LW. *Disenrollment Experience in the Medicare HMO and CMP Risk Program: 1985–1988.* Washington, DC: U.S. Department of Health and Human Services, 1990.

Thiemann DR, Coresh J, Oetgen WJ, et al. The association between hospital volume and survival after acute myocardial infarction in elderly patients. *New England Journal of Medicine* 340(21):1640–1648, 1999.

Torrance GW. Utility approach to measuring health-related quality of life. *Journal of Chronic Disease* 40:593–600, 1987.

Van Nostrand JF. *Common Beliefs About the Rural Elderly: What Do National Data Tell Us?* Hyattsville, MD: National Center for Health Statistics, 1993.

Vayda E. Operations in USA, Canada and UK. *New England Journal of Medicine* 288(10):527, 1973.

Ware JE, Sherbourne CD. The MOS 36-item short-form health survey (SF-36): I. Conceptual framework and item selection. *Medical Care* 27:473–483, 1992.

Weiner JP, Dobson A, Maxwell S, et al. Risk-adjusted Medicare capitation rates using ambulatory and inpatient diagnoses. *Health Care Financing Review* 17(3):77–99, 1996a.

Weiner JP, Parente ST, Garnick DW, et al. Variation in office based quality: A claims based profile of care provided to Medicare patients with diabetes. *Journal of the American Medical Association* 273(19):1503–1508, 1995.

Weiner JP, Starfield BH, Powe NR, et al. Ambulatory care practice variation within a Medicaid program. *Health Services Research* 30(6):751–770, 1996b.

REFERENCES

Weiner JP, Starfield BH, Steinwachs DM, et al. Development and application of a population-oriented measure of ambulatory care case-mix. *Medical Care* 29:452–472, 1991.

Wennberg JE. Dealing with medical practice variations: A proposal for action. *Health Affairs* 3(2):6–32, 1984.

Wennberg JE. Practice variations: Why all the fuss? *Internist* 26(4):6–8, 1985a.

Wennberg JE. Variation in medical practice and hospital costs. *Connecticut Medicine* 49(7):44–53, 1985b.

Wennberg JE. Setting outcome-based standards for carotid endarterectomy. *Journal of the American Medical Association* 256(18):2566–2567, 1986.

Wennberg JE, Gittelsohn A. Small area variations in health care delivery. *Science* 142:1102–1108, 1973.

White RE, Skipper BJ, Applegate WB, et al. Ordering decision and clinic cost variation among resident physicians. *Western Journal of Medicine* 141:117–122, 1984.

Woolhandler S, Himmelstein DU. Reverse targeting of preventive care due to lack of health insurance. *Journal of the American Medical Association* 25(19):2872–2874, 1988.

World Health Organization. *Ottawa Charter for Health Promotion.* Ottawa, Ontario: Canadian Public Health Association, 1986.

World Health Organization. *ICIDH-2: International Classification of Impairments, Activities, and Participation. A Manual of Dimensions of Disablement and Functioning. Beta-1 Draft for Field Trials.* Geneva: World Health Organization, 1997.

APPENDIX A

Workshop to Define Serious or Complex Medical Conditions

The committee convened a workshop on June 14, 1999, to elicit the knowledge, expertise, and opinions of professionals with involvement in issues associated with serious or complex medical conditions. Seven individuals were recruited to participate in a panel discussion of these issues. Presenters included Jeff Crowley, M.P.H., deputy executive director for programs at the National Association of People with AIDS and cochair of the health task force of the Consortium for Citizens with Disabilities; John Durant, M.D., executive vice president for the Association of Clinical Oncology; Joanne Lynn, M.D., director of the Center to Improve Care of the Dying, and Americans for Better Care of the Dying; Kathleen Brody, project director for model care of Kaiser Permanente; Helen Smits, M.D., president and chair of Healthright, Inc.; Lynn Etheredge, Ph.D., health care consultant; and Stan Jones, health care consultant.

The workshop provided the committee with the opportunity to benefit from the expertise of the panel members on a number of issues. Discussions addressed suggested definitions for serious or complex medical conditions and the impact of such definitions on specific patient populations including the disabled, cancer patients, and the elderly. A system for screening elderly patients for frailty was explored in detail, including the feasibility of generalizing such a system to other patient populations. The workshop presentations also provided a detailed analysis of the potential impact of the proposed regulations for Medicare+Choice on health care plans and opportunities to discuss issues of reimbursement and ensuring quality of care for patients with serious or complex conditions. The workshop was successful in stimulating questions and ideas among committee members, panel members, and workshop participants. Biographical sketches for each presenter can be found in Appendix B, a copy of the workshop agenda in Appendix C, and a list of workshop participants in Appendix D.

CLINICAL IMPLICATIONS OF DEFINING SERIOUS OR COMPLEX MEDICAL CONDITIONS

The first panel of speakers addressed the clinical implications of defining serious or complex medical conditions for specific populations including the disabled, cancer patients, and chronically ill patients with one or more comorbid conditions. These discussions provided the committee with a perspective on the unique health care needs of these populations and how these needs might best be integrated with the Consumers' Bill of Rights and the regulations concerning access to care proposed for the Medicare+Choice program. Panel presenters were Jeff Crowley, M.P.H.; John Durant, M.D.; and Joanne Lynn, M.D.

Disabled Populations

Mr. Crowley emphasized the need for a definition that encompasses the changing and diverse needs of people with disabilities. He emphasized three major points for the committee's consideration. First, the purpose of the definition of serious or complex medical condition must be clearly articulated. Second, any definition of serious or complex medical condition must be inherently flexible and must encompass a diversity of individuals and types of services and health care needs. The third and last point emphasized by Mr. Crowley was the need for a definition that will lead to improvements in the quality of care received by people with such conditions.

Mr. Crowley then elaborated on each of these three points. The purpose of the definition must be clearly articulated. People with disability already have experience with definitions. In fact, currently there are definitions of disability that cause many people to suspect that no good can come from creating some new definition. This is due, in part, to the fact that eligibility for cash assistance programs, such as Social Security income, the Supplemental Security Income program, and the Social Security Disability Income program, relies on a definition of disability that precludes the ability to be gainfully employed in the national economy. The narrow perspective of this definition can pose serious impediments for some people with disabilities to qualify for these income assistance programs and, subsequently, to qualify for Medicaid or Medicare health benefits.

An alternative definition of disability has been promulgated by the Americans with Disabilities Act, which asserts that a person is disabled if he or she has a substantial impairment that limits one or more major life activities. Advocates have generally felt this definition to be more acceptable, but since the law was enacted in 1990, employers and others who are subject to this law have challenged it. Questions have been raised about whether the definition of disability in the Americans with Disabilities Act includes people with asymptomatic HIV infection, people in the early stages of multiple sclerosis, or people with conditions that can be mitigated by fitting them with devices such as contact lenses for legally blind persons. The Supreme Court is just beginning to address these issues. It heard the first case in the last term, and ruled that a woman with asymptomatic HIV was disabled under the Americans with Disabilities Act. To summarize, persons with disabilities are somewhat hesitant accepting definitions of disability that may result in the loss of legal protections to ensure access to health care and other services that are needed.

Mr. Crowley also acknowledged the work of the President's Advisory Commission on Consumer Protection and Quality in the Health Care Industry. This commission focused specifically on issues associated with ensuring direct access to physician specialists by persons with a serious or complex medical condition. Mr. Crowley urged the committee to consider definitions of serious or complex medical conditions that extend beyond the particular issue of access to specialists. Ideally, the committee would develop a definition of serious or complex medical conditions that identifies persons for whom the absence of high-quality care has the potential to lead to a significant deterioration of their health status or quality of life or to prevent them from improving their health status. The committee was urged to establish a definition of serious or complex medical conditions that would guarantee access to the highest level of care that can be reasonably provided, including access to qualified, trained, and experienced providers. Experienced providers are a critical element in ensuring people get care that is consistent with current generally accepted standards of care.

Mr. Crowley also emphasized the need for a definition of serious and complex medical conditions that is inherently flexible and capable of encompassing a broad diversity of individuals and types of service and health care needs. About 54 million people in the United States live with disabilities, and they are incredibly diverse in both the severity of their conditions and the types of services and support they require. The committee was urged to consider this diversity as it seeks to define what constitutes a serious or complex medical condition. Specifically, consideration should be given to people with mental retardation, cerebral palsy, epilepsy, muscular dystrophy, and cystic fibrosis, as well as persons who are blind or deaf, people living with HIV, and persons who are paralyzed. Recognition of this diversity requires that the committee also acknowledge the following:

1. all of these conditions manifest themselves across a range of severity;
2. there is a broad range of service needs among these people;
3. assessment of the ability to perform activities of daily living or instrumental activities of daily living fails to capture all disabling conditions;
4. some disabilities are episodic in nature, and persons can go through periods when they appear completely healthy, only to experience intermittent periods of serious illness;
5. not all disabilities stem from illness; and finally,
6. illness does not always progress in a predictable manner.

Acknowledging these points requires the development of a definition of serious or complex medical conditions that is sufficiently broad to cover all people with disabilities for whom the absence of high-quality care holds the potential to lead to a significant deterioration of their health status or quality of life or to prevent them from improving their health status.

Mr. Crowley strongly recommended that the committee not attempt to craft a definition that is categorical in nature. Rather, the committee was urged to look closely at the experiences of people with disabilities to develop a definition that can accommodate persons with the same condition at different stages of disease progression or different levels of severity. In addition, such a definition should not create differential access to treatment based on the stage of illness. A number of problems would be created if a definition of serious and complex medical conditions was crafted such that a person would be covered only if he or she was experiencing an acute episode of illness. In addition, measures such as activities of daily living or instrumental activities of daily living can help determine if someone does have a serious or complex condition. However, the failure to be categorized as disabled by one of these measures should not be seen as an exclusionary criterion for having a serious or complex condition. Such a categorical definition could preclude, for example, people in the early stage of HIV, and people with multiple sclerosis, epilepsy, or a variety of other conditions, from receiving the care they need.

Mr. Crowley then went on to clarify that his remarks were intended to address special protections for people with serious or complex conditions to ensure that they receive the full spectrum and quality of services to sustain the highest level of health status and functioning. In fact, it is equally important that there be some mechanism for limiting who falls into this category, which raises the issue of defining medical necessity.

A solid definition of medical necessity can ensure that the diversity of people with disabilities get the care they need. It can also help place limits on care so that only persons for whom such care is necessary receive it.

The Centers for Disease Control and Prevention has a definition of medical necessity that might provide guidance for the development of a national standard for both public and private health care programs. Under this definition of medical necessity, health plans would be required to cover services that:

1. are calculated to prevent, diagnose, correct, or ameliorate a physical or mental condition that threatens life; causes pain or suffering; or results in illness, disability, or infirmity; or to maintain or preclude deterioration of health or functional ability;

2. are individualized, specific, and consistent with symptoms or confirmed diagnosis of the illness, disability, or injury under treatment and do not exceed the individual's needs;

3. are necessary and consistent with generally accepted professional medical standards as determined by the Secretary of Health and Human Services or by state departments of health; and

4. reflect the level of service that can be safely provided, for which no equally effective treatment is available.

Mr. Crowley reemphasized to the committee the importance of establishing a definition for serious or complex medical conditions that would result in improvements in the quality of care received by people with such conditions. Once a definition has been selected, coordinated efforts must be made to ensure that persons with such conditions are guaranteed access to the highest level of care that can reasonably be provided—including access to qualified, trained, and experienced providers—and that is consistent with current generally accepted standards of care. This has the potential to produce some measurable improvement in the health status of people with serious or complex medical conditions. In order to achieve this, more than a definition is needed. It will be of equal importance to develop mechanisms for monitoring health care delivery as it relates to people with serious or complex medical conditions. Such efforts might involve the development of a disability-specific Health Plan Employer Data and Information Set. If the Health Care Financing Administration (HCFA) is serious about using a definition of serious or complex medical conditions, it will have to develop a strategy for collecting information regarding how well health plans provide care to people such conditions. Most likely this will require the development of a new construct for tracking health plan performance. In addition to tracking how health plans are performing, it is also important to establish new expectations. To date, most expectations established for health plans have related to minimal standards of care and services that would be available to all enrollees in different types of plans. Establishing a definition of serious or complex medical conditions can allow the bar to be set higher for what is expected of health plans for people with these conditions. This means that a great deal of work will have to go into the development of performance and outcomes measures relating to individual categories of persons with these conditions, as well as measures that can monitor health plan performance in the aggregate for people with serious or complex conditions.

In response to questions from committee members, Mr. Crowley elaborated on several of his remarks. Emphasis was placed on developing a flexible definition for serious or complex medical conditions in order to prevent the problems from developing in areas such as the current context of health care delivery, regulatory expectations, and performance monitoring. Mr. Crowley clarified his belief that not all persons with disabilities should be considered to have a serious or complex medical condition. The tenet of medical necessity should serve as a check to ensure that inappropriate services or overuse of services will not occur. Mr. Crowley expressed the belief that some health plans have tried to minimize costs by essentially restricting everybody to primary care providers. However, for certain illnesses such as HIV, it has been demonstrated that a person will live longer if he or she has access to an experienced provider. It is necessary early on to provide access to specialized care for most people with disabilities. This is not to say that everyone needs to have a specialist as his or her primary care provider. It is most important that disabled persons receive treatments that are consistent with evidence-based clinical practice guidelines and ensure access to experienced providers.

Complexities of Patients with Cancer

Dr. Durant's opening comments reminded the committee that cancer is a complex of 100 or more diseases and that it is a disease of the genes, either inherited or acquired through susceptibility to various events in one's life. Cancer is probably the most difficult problem encountered in humans in terms of understanding its pathobiology, its origins, and its course. It is a group of diseases of which, in the early 1960s, one person in three could look forward to being cured. Today, slightly more than one person in two can expect to be cured. These numbers represent people who are free of disease for 5 years. Most people with most cancers who survive free of disease for 5 years are cured of their disease.

There are two extremely important things that must be done at the very beginning of the course of management. The first is a pathologic diagnosis, and the second is staging, including the use of molecular markers. Dr. Durant emphasized that neither of these activities should be left to amateurs. He cited a recent report to the Institute of Medicine by Hillner and Smith (Institute of Medicine, 1999) that demonstrated a clear dose-response curve between the experience of the health care provider and patient outcomes with a wide variety of cancers, stage for stage. That is, the survival of patients with a particular cancer improved significantly when they received care from practitioners with a large volume of experience in treating that type of cancer. Most cases of cancer require multidisciplinary evaluation from the outset. This usually means two or three or more people knowledgeable in the particular cancer, and in many cases treatment involves more than one discipline in a planned, prospective fashion.

It is very important to understand that there is usually only one chance to cure the patient, and this is the first chance. After this, so-called salvage therapy may induce responses but, with only a few exceptions, does result in a cure. Exceptions to this rule include acute leukemia, where repeat treatment—usually a transplant—is sometimes very effective in children. Similarly, Hodgkin's disease, some lymphomas, and testicular cancer may yield to the second or third retreatment. Other than these types of cancer, with very few exceptions the first chance is the only chance.

Dr. Durant also pointed out a societal problem with these numbers and the treatment and chance for cure. Specifically, he noted large gaps in survival rates for parts of our culture. African Americans and Hispanics, in particular, do not seem to do as well, probably for a variety of complex reasons. For example, black men with prostate cancer don't do nearly as well as white men. Black men with colon cancer do much less well than white men, and less well even than black women. Palliative care, including some specific cancer therapies, may improve the survival time, as well as increase the quality of life, but it is almost never curative.

Early detection of a malignancy clearly improves chances for survival in the initial episode, but early detection of a recurrence does not improve chances for survival. Thus, it makes great sense to treat and cure at the time of the initial diagnosis, because all the strategies that have been employed for picking up recurrences early have resulted in increased survival rates.

It is important to note that cured patients are at much higher risk for second malignancies than people who never had a malignancy. With the recent interest in breast cancer, it is fairly clear that the greatest risk is having had breast cancer before. This does not represent a metastasis of the initial cancer. Rather, it is a second breast cancer. The greatest risk for aero-digestive cancer is to have had a previous one from which you were cured. There are not many cancers in the aero-digestive system that yield to salvage therapy. Some patients with early larynx cancer may be cured if radiation therapy fails by laryngectomy, but most of the time the greatest problem is the development of another primary cancer.

Despite the medical and technological advances of the past 25 or 30 years, it is still very difficult to tell which patients in a clinically similar group will do well. We have some general prognostic characteristics for virtually all sites. However, if one considers all women diagnosed with breast cancer and three positive nodes, it is very difficult to be sure which of these women will be cured and which will not. All of this means that experience and intuitions are sometimes helpful, but patients require some kind of follow-up until they are "out of the woods."

The management of cancer patients in the initial episode is well illustrated by pediatric oncology. Undergoing complicated, vigorous treatment at the time of the initial diagnosis cures most children diagnosed with cancer today. Indeed, most patients who are children enter clinical trials. This is an example of a care or treatment plan. A clinical trial is a method for ensuring accountability and responsibility for outcomes by being able to compare responses to treatment between apparently similar patients.

In short, cancer is a complicated disease or set of diseases. We are in the middle of learning a lot more about them, but we are a long way from a complete understanding of risk factors, treatments, and prevention of recurrences. There are a couple of cancers that are not complex and serious and are also fairly common. One of them is cervical intraepithelial neoplasia (CIN). When it is not invasive, this condition is not considered a cancer; it is usually manageable by very simple means in a gynecologist's office and does not require inpatient treatment. Spread of this type of cancer to other organs, however, places the patient at significantly increased risk of morbidity and mortality.

Another very common set of cancers that are not serious or complex are basal and squamous cell cancers of the skin. Once in a while, one of these forms of skin cancer spreads to surrounding tissues. This usually, perhaps invariably, occurs because the patient has neglected an obvious problem. However, these cancers are rarely serious or complex because they do not metastasize.

According to the 50,000 members of all the clinical oncologic societies in this country, the initial evaluation of a patient and the treatment plan should be the result of the work of an interdisciplinary team of experts who individually have large volumes of experience with the disease. Dr. Durant again cited the Hillner and Smith report to the Institute of Medicine (Institute of Medicine, 1999) documenting clear dose–response curves between experience and survival.

In his concluding remarks, Dr. Durant encouraged the committee to be flexible in developing definitions for serious or complex medical conditions. He also emphasized that there are important behaviors that influence the outcome for a fraction of patients who would benefit most from having care provided by experienced specialists at the time of the initial diagnosis.

In response to a question about strategies to treat the third or fourth recurrence of a cancer and defining when the benefits of therapy, particularly aggressive therapy, outweigh the human and financial costs, Dr. Durant indicated that the medical oncology community has few guidelines. There is, however, one exception in this area, which concerns the management of advanced stage, non-small-cell lung cancer. Currently accepted guidelines support one chemotherapeutic regimen for patients with advanced disease. There is significant clinical evidence demonstrating the efficacy of this type of intervention. A poor response to this single treatment regimen would be followed by palliative care or participation in a clinical trial with a new agent if one was available. Dr. Durant urged the committee to be aware that treatment guidelines for most cancer patients rely on successful intervention at the time of initial diagnosis. Repeating treatments can cure very few people, and the likelihood of cure for persons with advanced disease at initial diagnosis or point of recurrence is very low.

Dr. Durant also noted that geographic differences in treatment patterns and survival rates are well documented, with generally poorer outcomes for those treated in rural settings. Religious, cultural, and attitudinal factors contribute to such disparities in outcome. However, it is highly unlikely that practitioners in a rural community will see the volume of patients required to learn how to successfully manage different cancers. Dr. Durant urged that such patients be transported to a medical center that has a high volume of patients and concomitantly higher levels of practitioner experience. The Hillner and Smith report (Institute of Medicine, 1999) did not indicate that such a setting had to be an academic medical center; it just needed to be a medical center with a lot of experience. The report indicated that improved survival was first noted when the number of cases treated at a facility reached 50 and that, for every increment in patient volume, there was no plateau reached for experience and improved outcome.

In response to a question about follow-up care to be provided after the 5-year window for survival, Dr. Durant indicated that most oncologists prefer that such patients return to their primary care physicians. They should then return at yearly intervals for a follow-up visit with the oncology specialist because of the potential for another cancer. In his concluding remarks, Dr. Durant supported the notion that Medicare should provide funding for controlled clinical trials, since in a number of disease areas it probably provides the best type of care. He noted that the Association of Clinical Oncology espouses the viewpoint that clinical trials represent a standard of care. If the trial is well constructed and is conducted in an ethically responsible manner, patients will get no less than the best and they might get better than the best.

Serious and Complex Chronic Illness at the End of Life

The remarks of Mr. Crowley and Dr. Durant were complemented by those of Dr. Joanne Lynn, director of the Center to Improve Care of the Dying and Americans for Better Care of the Dying. Her presentation focused on the relevance of the category of serious or complex medical conditions to the delivery of health care. She suggested that the language of the health care delivery system is terribly important, especially since constructs that lack labels are frequently overlooked or ignored. For example, traditional labels for health care delivery include inpatient hospital care; outpatient, ambulatory care from physicians; home health care; long-term care, and so forth. Then medical and nursing knowledge is categorized by diagnoses such as hypertension, diabetes, cancer of various kinds, and cardiopulmonary disorders. As a result of characterizing the health care delivery system by the environment in which care is delivered and by the diagnosis of disease, a specialist is defined as someone who is very good at delivering care in one or two environments such as the hospital and the physician's office. In addition, a specialist would have expertise in caring for a specific diagnosis or a group of related diagnoses. However, the current health care delivery system has not recognized a specialized service that works primarily to provide long-term care to persons with multiple diagnoses. With respect to long-term care for populations with serious chronic disease served by Medicare, it is most common for individuals to have health care needs that cross multiple delivery environments and require specialists to care for four or five different diseases, through to death.

Dr. Lynn pointed out that current research on the health care delivery system is often limited in focus to populations with only a single disease. For example, the median age of cancer patients enrolled in studies is 60 or 62 years. However, the mean age at death from cancer is significantly older. In addition, virtually all of the studies are limited to people with one disease. Frequently, individuals with dementia, serious comorbidities, or physical access barriers to participation are excluded from studies of the health care delivery system. This results in an emphasis of research on patient populations limited to a single care environment or diagnosis.

Dr. Lynn identified a need for research that will accommodate both multiple care environments and multiple diseases. Specialty care is necessary to address all the health care needs of people with, for example, breast cancer, older age, physical frailty, a bad hip, a bad heart, hearing disorders, low socioeconomic status, and a fragmented social support system. According to Dr. Lynn, dealing with these complex cases requires specialized care, although no such specialty is currently recognized by the American Board of Medical Specialists. A team of professionals with some interlocking medical disciplines and expertise would most effectively deliver such specialty care.

Unfortunately, the structure of traditional Medicare fee-for-service payments encourages fragmentation rather than integration of care. Medicare managed care plans have the potential to offer integrated specialty care for patients with long-term health needs. However, a variety of social and political forces have prevented widespread integration of this type of system of service delivery for long-term care by Medicare managed care plans. Furthermore, few individuals have developed the comprehensive expertise to manage complex, long-term care for patients with multiple diagnoses. There are a very few exceptions to this. One is hospice, which provides care for about 20 percent of the population for, on average, the final month preceding death. Similarly, the Program of All-Inclusive Care for the Elderly takes care of about 10,000 elderly people across the country. There are also some other very small programs, often in older staff model health maintenance organizations such as Kaiser or Group Health, in which patients with multiple diagnoses or comorbidities receive multidisciplinary team care that integrates their physical, social, emotional, and mental health needs. This type of integrated, team-based care should be considered a specialty on its own, and delivery of such care probably underlies potential definitions and treatment plans for serious and complex illness.

Dr. Lynn pointed out that several categories or groups emerge when the health of the general population is considered. One group includes a minority of persons with no particular health care needs at all, or those who shun health care because of religious persuasion or similar reasons. A second, much larger group is comprised of people who have minor, intermittent acute care and preventive health needs. This includes the majority of the American population. The third category consists of individuals who, on any given day, are ill with a condition that requires known and accepted medical intervention(s) to restore health. On the whole, these are sick people who are going to get well, such as individuals with peptic ulcer disease or those who are seen in the emergency room after, or while suffering a heart attack.

Finally, there is a category that includes people with conditions that can be considered serious and complex because there is no therapeutic regimen that will make them fully well again. However, interventions are available to help these individuals maintain a role in society despite having a disability or chronic health condition that will persist until death. The paradigm case might be persons who are born with moderate to severe mental retardation. They are going to live with this disability for the duration of their lives. However, if they receive good support for their physical, social, emotional, and mental health, the impact on their life span will be moderate, if at all.

In contrast, there are people with serious and complex conditions that will worsen over time and eventually result in death. For example, vascular surgery can be performed on an individual who experiences a heart attack. This individual is diagnosed with mild heart failure and, with good medical management, might live another 20 years. However, the person has now been diagnosed with a disease that cannot be cured and most likely will be the eventual cause of death unless he or she develops a more serious, life-threatening health condition or experiences a serious trauma or injury. In fact, the number of persons with such serious and complex medical conditions is growing. The median age of adults at death is 80. Most people are diagnosed with a few serious illnesses before they reach the end of their lives. For example, the average woman now has 5 years of disability before death while the average man survives with 3 years of disability before dying. Most of these years of disability are due to complications arising from the disease that will ultimately result in death. The exceptions to this are arthritic and osteoporotic conditions that can cause significant disability but are not primary causes of death. In summary, serious and complex medical conditions can include those illnesses that cause progressive deterioration in health status over time and frequently require care from multiple specialties including health, emotional, social, and mental interventions.

Dr. Lynn also emphasized that the medical community currently is not able to make accurate predictions about when persons with serious or complex conditions are likely to die. In reviewing relevant data, Dr. Lynn and her associates found that on the day preceding death, the median lung cancer patient had a 20 percent likelihood of surviving for 2 more months. Similarly, 1 week prior to death from lung cancer, the median patient had an estimated 50 percent chance of living 2 additional months (Lynn et al., 1997). In fact, tracking the experience of persons with cancer indicates that 20 to 30 percent actually die quite suddenly. These individuals are very sick and frail with their disease, but they are functioning with an acceptable degree of health that gives no indication that death could be imminent. This level of function, however, is abruptly compromised by events such as development of a pulmonary embolus, infection, or other acute complications, one of which ultimately results in a rather sudden death during the course of a chronic disease.

Review of mortality data for patients suffering from congestive heart failure suggests a similar pattern (Lynn et al., 1997). For example, on the day preceding death, the median patient with congestive heart failure still has a 50 percent chance to survive an additional 6 months. One week prior to death, this patient has approximately an 80 percent likelihood of surviving 6 months, despite that fact that such individuals live for a long time with severe compromises to their cardiovascular and respiratory health. In fact, patients with cancer, congestive heart disease, and similar health conditions survive for quite a long time with significant functional disabilities.

The data indicate that for most patients with cancer, the process of dying is usually confined to the last 6 or 8 weeks. However, most patients with serious or complex health problems are severely disabled for a long period of time. They experience intermittent, acute health threats (called exacerbations of disease) that are medically managed with good recovery until one particular complication causes death. However, at the beginning of the week prior to death, no one could have predicted the death in that particular week because the disability associated with the disease had been present and unchanged for a long time.

Patients with serious or complex medical conditions have disease of long duration, episodic crises and exacerbation of disease, and significant, long-term disability. They may require a type of specialty care that presents a very different challenge to our current health care system. The need for such specialized care has emerged only over the past 20 years as medical knowledge and technology have led to the development of interventions that are capable of sustaining life for patients with chronic, disabling conditions for long periods of time. It is no longer the exception, but the rule, that people with significant compromises to their health live for a long time postdiagnosis due to advances in technology and medical management interventions. There is a need for a specialization or area of specialty care to attend to the long-term and diverse needs of these patient populations.

Dr. Lynn then suggested the following definitions for serious and complex conditions. Serious medical conditions would include those that are substantially disabling, progressive, and eventually fatal. Complex conditions would require services in a variety of domains or disciplines for the person to live well in the time preceding death. Examples of programs that have used these or similar definitions include the following:

1. Franklin Health. Patients with serious or complex illnesses are targeted for intensive personal care management, with results demonstrating significant improvements in the value of care services.

2. Franciscan Health System, Tacoma, Washington. This program identifies patients in general medicine with a "surprise" question (is this patient sick enough that you would not be surprised he or she died in a few months?). The program targets advanced planning and community care coordination, which in turn lead to dramatic improvements in patient satisfaction, use of hospice care, and deaths at home.

3. Medicare Expenditures. Following hospitalization for a serious or complex illness such as congestive heart failure or chronic obstructive pulmonary disease, ongoing payments for care average about $24,000 per year until death. Patients in these cohorts are identified by one serious exacerbation of their illness and a simple physiological test such as an echocardiogram for congestive heart failure or blood gas for chronic obstructive pulmonary disease.

Dr. Lynn advocated that serious or complex medical conditions be used as a category in three ways. The first use of the category is to trigger direct access to specialist care that can be defined as "a health care practitioner, facility, or center . . . that has adequate expertise through appropriate training and experience to provide high-quality care in treating the condition." The second use would be as a substitute for the continuity-of-care provisions that are currently extended to those with terminal illness. Patients with a serious and complex condition such as congestive heart failure are terribly disabled and should be protected from suddenly losing their provider, as are those with terminal illness in the Consumers' Bill of Rights and Responsibilities. A third use is as protections to ensure that suitable specialist(s) are eligible to provide care under a particular Medicare+Choice plan, will take new patients, and are willing to take a particular patient with a serious or complex condition. The provider must be accessible and acceptable to the patient.

Finally, Dr Lynn discussed insights gleaned from quality improvement work in this area. Patients with serious or complex conditions can be identified with meaningful administrative and clinical criteria. For example, congestive heart failure might qualify with one hospitalization for failure and an echocardiogram to document an ejection fraction less than 30 percent or severe diastolic dysfunction. Insights on the qualifying thresholds and the standards of practice will arise from research on variation in treatment practices for such conditions, along with efforts to identify better or best-practice guidelines and evidence of substantial improvements in the quality and standardization of care.

Dr. Lynn was asked by the committee to elaborate further upon guidance she would suggest to HCFA with respect to providing access to specialized care versus access to specialists. In reply, Dr. Lynn cited the model provided by hospice where the physician specialty is almost irrelevant. Dr. Lynn also referenced several Senate bills, which suggest ways to define specialists, such as Senate bill 6, proposed by Senators Daschle, Kennedy, and others. This bill defines the term "specialist" for a specific health condition as a health care practitioner, facility, or center, such as a Center of Excellence, that has adequate expertise through appropriate training and experience to provide high quality care in treating the condition. Dr. Lynn concurred with such a definition for specialists and went on to clarify that a new understanding is necessary to determine what type of specialist(s) is needed to take care of patients with serious and complex health problems. Given the complexity of care needs among these patients, it is unlikely that a single specialty, selected from the current list of medical specialties, is adequate. Currently, a 92-year-old woman with 16 different diagnoses and no income is unlikely to receive the type of coordinated care that would be necessary to sustain her life. Similarly, there is a large and growing group of people with serious and complex conditions involving multiple diagnoses and multidisciplinary care for which no single existing medical specialty has been defined. On the other hand, a patient with one discrete diagnosis, such as ovarian cancer, can be reasonably well assured that she will receive the current standards of care for her disease from one medical specialty such as oncology or gynecologic oncology.

Dr. Lynn was also asked to provide her thoughts about the inclusion of people with mental retardation in the larger group of people with serious and complex conditions who require multispecialty care. The committee pointed out that for persons with mental retardation, it is often the nonmedical specialties that are most critical to their being able to at least maintain their functional status.

Dr. Lynn pointed out that a single specialist often handles acute care health crises well with little or no regard to interpersonal skills, continuity of care, and other related issues. In contrast, persons living with a progressively worsening chronic condition such as heart disease, chronic obstructive pulmonary disease, or cancer have a very different set of needs. These include the following:

1. good medical treatment with a focus on prevention of disease exacerbation, improvement of overall functional status, and survival and comfort;
2. good symptom control or management;
3. a care management system that offers continuity, coordination, and comprehensiveness;
4. clearly stated and understood expectations by patients and family members of what is likely to occur during the course of the illness;
5. customized care that reflects the preferences of the patient and family members;
6. support for the physical, psychological, social, and spiritual needs of the patient and family members in order to maximize the quality of each day; and
7. judicious use of society's resources.

A team of specialists, including a physician, is necessary to accomplish these seven diverse needs. However, a nurse, social worker, or physician can lead the team. There has to be a helpful doctor in the team mix. Dr. Lynn pointed out that teams that are not dominated by doctors often provide much greater assistance to families and children coping with serious illness or mental retardation than physician-led teams. Doctors may be present, but they are not the dominant force. Living with serious disease is the challenge, rather than fixing or curing such disease.

Dr. Lynn was also asked to clarify the point at which an illness becomes serious and complex since such illnesses begin to accumulate as people age. This was noted to present a wide zone of clinical uncertainty. It was Dr. Lynn's opinion that data systems and analysis are not yet available to provide a clear response to this question. She did suggest, however, that four kinds of illness are largely responsible for 90 percent of the deaths in the Medicare population: (1) cancer; (2) heart and lung failure; (3) dementia and stroke; and (4) frailty of advanced old age. Dr. Lynn suggested that it is fairly easy to determine a threshold for each of these conditions. For example, the threshold for congestive heart failure might be one exacerbation, hospitalization for failure, and ejection fractions of less than 30 percent or diastolic dysfunction. The threshold for dementia might be immobility and incontinence.

Such thresholds could be established for the primary diseases leading to death. In addition, overall well-being or functional status could be assessed by inability to exercise at a certain level, inability to ambulate a certain distance, and so forth. This would ensure the inclusion of persons who do not meet the disease-specific thresholds but are, for some reason, self-care disabled. These thresholds would be the cutpoints for determining when individuals are considered to have a serious or complex medical condition. It would then be necessary to define the service array to meet the comprehensive care needs of this cohort, which would likely include the seven needs identified earlier. This could then be coordinated with determination of the right price to provide the requisite care, as well as regulations to support implementation of the care plan.

Dr. Lynn suggested that defining the characteristics that result in classifying a condition as a serious or complex as well as identification of the array of required services, would in turn facilitate efforts to determine the right price for care delivery to these patient populations. For example, improved financing might be a risk adjustment or a rate for the Program of All-Inclusive Care for the Elderly or an appropriate reimbursement rate in the VERA system at the Veterans Administration. She suggested that risk adjustment, which has already been used with some success, might be a viable alternative for determination of price. As an example, Dr. Lynn proposed application of the currently accepted risk adjusters for congestive heart failure at the first episode of illness exacerbation and when the patient met the ejection fraction criteria, rather than in the next fiscal year. The risk adjustment rates could be provided to the managed care company from that point on until death. This would prevent having to retrigger the rate at least once a year with subsequent hospitalizations. This rate could support the development of some terrific service arrays for a disease that accounts for 25 percent of all deaths.

An urban setting could support a comprehensive health care delivery team that really knew how to take good care of congestive heart failure, for example, if the providers of care could make a living at it. Dr. Lynn further suggested that many patients have both chronic obstructive pulmonary disease and congestive heart failure, with cigarette smoking the dominant etiology. It is likely that the same service provider group would take care of these patients as well. Different teams might work with dementia.

From HCFA's perspective, all that is necessary would be to define the service array through regulation and rate of payment after the criteria for identifying patient cohorts with serious and complex conditions have been determined. Identifying when patients cross the threshold of having a serious and complex condition also generally identifies a population in the last 1 or 2 years of life. These patients drain resources significantly, yet are also frequently dissatisfied with the quality of care they receive. In fact, such patients require a specialized array of services to cope with all aspects of their illness, and these can be provided most efficiently and cost-effectively when a multidisciplinary, experienced team assumes responsibility for care.

In a final question from the audience, Dr. Lynn was asked if she thought it was possible to develop definitions and arrays of service only for serious or complex conditions or for thousands of conditions based on the International Classification of Diseases, Ninth and Tenth Editions (ICD-9 and ICD-10), which affect great numbers of people. Dr. Lynn concurred that as the population continues to age, the need for multidisciplinary care services by teams will increase. For example, 80 percent of the people on Medicare who die have one of five diagnoses within a year preceding death: heart disease, respiratory failure, cancer, dementia, or stroke. At this time, it appears that the service array is likely to be similar for each of these five conditions. Perhaps with 3 or 4 years of experience with this service array, special services for one or more of the diagnoses will be identified and advocated. Dr. Lynn suggested that rather than taking on all diagnoses, HCFA should focus on the major causes of morbidity, mortality, and resource utilization including heart and lung failure, cancer, stroke, dementia, and also frailty of old age. Frailty lacks an ICD-9 code, but it is likely that persons with very little physiological reserves and problems in five or six areas are not going to be able to handle an added acute health threat such as pneumonia. The frail elderly also deserve consideration as a serious and complex medical group requiring an appropriate array of treatment services led by a multidisciplinary team. Such services also merit efforts to determine appropriate pricing by a mechanism such as risk adjustment and regulation to support the service array and reimbursement plan.

Example of a Population-Based Screening Intervention for Care Delivery Integration

Kathleen Brody, P.H.N., is a public health nurse with 15 years experience working with the Social Health Maintenance Organization associated with Kaiser Permanente in Portland, Oregon. Since 1996, she has served as the Project Director for Project Seek (Screen Every Elder in Kaiser), also known as Kaiser Permanente's Medicare Screening Project. Her presentation provided the committee with an example of a population-based screening intervention, targeted to patients 65 years of age and older, to facilitate integration of care delivery.

In her opening remarks, Ms. Brody provided some background information on Kaiser's Social Health Maintenance Organization project, which is a national Medicare demonstration project designed to maintain frail elderly in their homes by providing comprehensive benefits that include home-based, long-term-care services. During the past 15 years, this project has relied on a self-report health status form in compliance with the mandate by HCFA that social health maintenance organizations collect self-report data from members about their health on an annual basis. Analysis of this information is intended to identify those who are at risk of nursing home placement and likely to need extra services to maintain stability in their home.

The initial health status form self-assessment tool started as a paper-and-pencil system and through the years evolved into a computerized, optical scan form. Some of the research base for the instrument had its roots in work completed by Douglas Reid and funded by the National Institute on Aging that examined relationships between depression and the use of antihypertensive drugs. Similarly, a study received resources from the Garfield Memorial Fund to support the development of a model that could correctly identify people who would be in need of daily assistance in order to continue to maintain themselves in their homes. In addition, there is a significant literature examining the relationship between identified risk and high utilization of services.

In 1990, Kaiser Permanente began to examine the model of care it was providing, which consisted basically of outpatient, ambulatory care services that plan members accessed when they felt they had a need. These needs were then assessed and treated. This was, and still is, the basic model of care for Kaiser. In the course of its analysis, however, Kaiser found that there was a cohort of people within its membership that the basic model of care delivery failed to serve adequately. This cohort included vulnerable patients who were no longer seeking active treatments to eliminate or improve their disease. It also included patients suffering simultaneously from a number of complex disease processes that could not all be addressed in ambulatory, outpatient care settings or whose totality of medical care needs required not only a physician but a complex medical health care team approach. Kaiser then defined these cohorts of patients as those at risk who are in need of a second model of care. That model of care would be a health care team approach that does active outreach to the members, especially those who are vulnerable and are not able to come into the medical office and seek care themselves.

In developing this second model of care, Kaiser proposed that a person could have any number of diseases or symptoms, and the model of care required would involve a person-based goal-setting process that incorporated all of the member's needs. It was then to be determined whether these needs could be met by the traditional model of self-care planning or alternatively, by a care management model which would rely on a case management approach.

The Health Status Form Questionnaire was examined to build an empiric model instrument, to predict elderly members at risk of frailty in the coming year. A total of 5,810 members returned completed questionnaires for a 92 percent response rate. The self-report data were supplemented by information from several Kaiser Permanente Northwest data systems, including the Pharmacy System Database; Admission, Discharge, and Transfer Database; Membership Information System Database; and Nursing Home Certification and Long-Term Home-Based Care Database.

The study design was a retrospective observation of a cross-sectional, 1-year sample. Self-report data were collected on day 1, and the observation period covered the next 365 days, during which episodes of frailty were noted. Frailty was defined as having one or more of three possible outcome events during the year. These events were (1) becoming certified for nursing home care, (2) having a nursing home admission, and (3) receiving home-based long-term-care services.

Applying a stepwise logistic regression model that relied on data from these various sources resulted in the identification of 13 variables statistically associated with frailty. These included the following:

1. assistance required for medication use,
2. assistance required for bathing,
3. assistance required for dressing skills,
4. prior nursing home use,

5. use of a wheelchair,
6. use of a bedside commode,
7. two or more hospital admissions,
8. self-report that health interferes with activities of daily living,
9. presence of four or more health conditions,
10. increasing age,
11. assistance required for eating,
12. poor health as compared with others, and
13. assistance required for managing money.

By applying the weights from the logistic regression model for these 13 variables, it was possible to identify more than one-half of the members who would experience frailty within the coming year. The sensitivity of the predictive model was 54.6 percent; more than half of the members who experienced frailty during the year were classified by the model using 13 Health Status Form Questionnaire variables. The specificity of the model was 97.9 percent. The false-positive rate was 18.1 percent, while the false-negative rate was 7.3 percent. The overall positive predictive value of the model was 81.9 percent.

Further analysis of the data revealed that four of the self-report variables (age, needing or receiving bathing assistance, needing or receiving assistance to take medications, and indicating that health conditions interfered with daily activities) explained 90 percent of the residual chi square from the intercept and classified persons almost as well as the total model of 13 variables. Specificity for the smaller model was identical to that for the 13-item model, and sensitivity decreased only 4 percent. The false-positive rate for the four-variable model decreased by 2.5 percent, and the false-negative rate increased only 0.6 percent. The positive predictive value for the four-variable model was 79.4 percent.

Kaiser Permanente Northwest was able to follow the entire test population of 5,810 at regular intervals as members moved into and out of all the silos of care settings. During the initial phase of this research in 1984 and 1985, patient enrollment in the study included a fairly healthy group of age-eligible Medicare beneficiaries. Now these members have aged into a cohort with a mean age of 83 years. This cohort looks similar to the projected older population for the United States by the year 2015. Analysis of the cohort provides a perspective on a microcosm of what it will look like in ambulatory care settings that deal with an aging population. Applying the age- and gender-specific rates of frailty for the Kaiser cohort and adjusting these rates to per-thousand population, a health maintenance organization in a different part of the country could disperse its own age-gender population and apply the age-adjusted rates to its members in order to determine within a given year how many members will experience frailty. This frailty cuts across disease strata including diagnoses of dementia, depression, and other types of disabilities. There is little variation in the distribution attributable to gender, but the distribution is extremely sensitive to age.

Ms. Brody then addressed the action items undertaken by Kaiser Permanente to put the Health Status Form Questionnaire in place at Kaiser sites across the United States. The Center for Health Research developed the information needed to disseminate the form to local Kaiser divisions so that it would influence care in medical offices and help to identify best practices. The coefficients of the model were applied to estimate a member's probability of frailty by taking these weightings and the intercept and creating a risk. Kaiser used 5 as the frailty cutoff, and that's how it determined the members it was looking for.

It was proposed that the Center for Health Research would mail forms to all new Medicare enrollees at participating Kaiser medical offices. As data are returned to the center, the information is analyzed and distributed to the local Kaiser markets. Member response rates to the Health Status Form Questionnaire range between 85 and 90 percent. The initial strategy for data collection and management was discussed at the Kaiser Interregional Committee on Aging in 1992 and resulted in funding for some pilot projects. By 1996, Southern California Kaiser, Orange County, began to utilize the services of the Center for Health Research. Now the data collection, management, and analysis by the Center for Health Research are conducted for Kaiser regions across the United States including the Southern California, Northern California, Rocky Mountain, Mid-Atlantic, Northwest, and Northeast regions.

Kaiser divisions participating in the Medicare Screening Project send their Medicare enrollment information, including address, age, and name information, to the Center for Health Research via e-mail. Mailing of the Health Status Form Questionnaires to new members is done on a monthly basis. Completed member questionnaires are received daily and scanned into a computer for analysis. The center completes a weekly summary report on all the data received, including information that can be used by Medicare managers and membership services departments on new deaths, new terminations, corrections in names and addresses, and so forth. In addition, each Kaiser site receives a software package through Microsoft Access. This software stores the aggregate data and produces single-page member summaries, which tell exactly what the member's responses were to the eight pages of questions on the Health Status Form Questionnaire.

Sites are encouraged to use information such as physician provider codes, facility codes, division codes, and so on, to facilitate aggregation of the data in a useful manner. These aggregate analyses produce additional reports for triaging and screening new enrollees. Needs for prevention services, acute care services, mental health services, and so on, are identified for each enrollee based on the self-reported responses to the questionnaire. This information is integrated into a care plan that is negotiated with the member and facilitates identification of priority concerns.

Use of information from the Health Status Form Questionnaire has improved the aggregate description of Kaiser's Medicare population, which in turn has improved efforts for planning and delivery of services. For example, a baseline description of the health and service utilization needs of each member is established at the point of enrollment. This information can be monitored over time to identify positive and negative changes in health status. The information assists in proactive treatment and patient triage to augment the standard medical care model. This information also helps the staff in medical offices to organize care and to improve the delivery of day-to-day health care services by identifying those patients with the most acute need. Medical staff can use this information to facilitate interactions during the patient's first visit to a physician. The physician is informed about major issues of concern prior to the patient interaction, and the patient does not have to repeat information captured by the Health Status Form Questionnaire.

On average, 5 percent of new enrollees are defined as currently frail or at risk of becoming in the next year. The identification of specific individuals at risk for frailty facilitates efforts by medical staff to establish complex plans of care and treatment. Having such plans ensures better coordination and continuity of care as the patient proceeds from one site of care to another.

Proposed next steps for the project include the following:

1. Design of a re-screening instrument and methodology to determine how many years it takes for the nonfrail to develop frailty: the cohort established for the Social Health Maintenance Organization will provide useful information to answer this question
2. Comparison of mortality rates between the frail and the nonfrail: initial analysis of the data indicates that almost 27 percent of the frail will die within 12 months of their being identified as frail.
3. Assessment of the development of new incidence of frailty among the nonfrail over a 10-year period of time: this will help determine the sensitivity and specificity of screening at different intervals such as 5, 3, and 2 years.
4. Initiation of contracts with other health care plans and service providers to screen their new enrollees in Medicare for frailty.

Committee members expressed a great deal of enthusiasm for Ms. Brody's presentation on Kaiser's Medicare Screening Project. One question of interest was whether the Health Status Form Questionnaire could be used to screen nonelderly enrollees in Medicare. It was pointed out that these patients might benefit from a similar type of screening and from development of the same type of care plan. Ms. Brody indicated that plans are underway to use the same instrument with the nonaged Medicare population. She cautioned that the frailty prediction score would not be available due to a lack of data and insufficient time to observe outcomes in this new population. She noted, however, that responses to the questionnaire would be useful to physicians and health care teams in order to provide a complete picture of nonelderly members of Medicare and facilitate the development of care and treatment plans that address a comprehensive set of patient needs.

One committee member noted that the type of screening conducted under the Kaiser model could yield two different outcomes. First, it could provide a tool and screening results that would allow plans to avoid patients with certain risk profiles. Alternatively, it could be a tool to identify risks and then couple the scores with an appropriate plan. As such, it would be part of efforts to conduct quality assessment of care plans. It was also noted that a similar screening effort was initiated by the OASIS project, which yielded a scale or score for physiological risk or functional assessment. A representative from HCFA indicated that initial difficulties with the Medicare Home Health Care Quality Assurance and Improvement Demonstration Outcome and Assessment Information Set (OASIS-B), concerning violation of patient privacy, had been overcome and the system was available for use. A comment was made that the OASIS project also provided the opportunity to collect data on risks and outcomes that could facilitate development of care plans and serve as an assessment of the effectiveness of these plans.

Ms. Brody was also asked if the interventions and care plans developed in response to results from the Health Status Form Questionnaire were mandated within the Kaiser system and subject to audit. In response, it was noted that Kaiser developed the Medicare Screening Project in response to some of the requirements of the Balanced Budget Act of 1997. It was felt that the screening effort had the potential to define a new target population and associated care plans that could be tracked though an audit trail. However, the development of the care plans is not yet a mandatory requirement for all Kaiser facilities. The specific elements of an appropriate care plan for elderly Medicare enrollees identified as at risk of frailty have not yet been determined, although efforts to do so are ongoing across the United States. There is some indication of the need to develop experts or specialty care services to deal with the needs of a geriatric population. This is particularly true as the number of aging Americans continues to increase in the coming decades. The screening effort raises clinicians' awareness of issues relevant to the care of this population. It also ensures that when a patient comes to a medical setting such as an ambulatory care center or emergency room, staff will have computer access to the patient's care plan. This is intended to maintain and improve the continuity of care for such patients.

The committee also discussed with Ms. Brody the issue of depression, which is one element of the calculated score for risk of frailty. Specifically, Ms. Brody was asked to describe the importance of depression in determining the overall level of disability. In response, Ms. Brody noted that the inability to deal with the chronicity of their disease over time presents a significant challenge to people who are having these slow transitions toward death. It was her opinion that depression, lack of motivation to engage in self-care, and decreased motivation and resilience in coping with the annoyances of living with chronic disease can build up over time. As support systems fail, loved ones die and resources diminish, depression seems to be more evident. The Health Status Form Questionnaire provides clinicians with specific information about depression. As a result, it can be included as an issue to be addressed by the care plan.

A final questioned was posed by one of the members of the workshop audience. The panel was asked if there was anything comparable to OASIS in home health care for the Medicare enrollee in managed care plans that would be based on a standardized needs assessment. It was noted that such an instrument would provide HCFA with an opportunity to compare the effectiveness of treatment between different plans. It was acknowledged that the Kaiser project was innovative and could provide a model for a methodology to identify at-risk patient populations and develop appropriate treatment plans, especially for more complicated, less profitable patient groups. Adaptation of the Kaiser methodology by HCFA could lead to much more effective treatments for patients with complex medical conditions, as well as the necessary financing and regulatory structure that is often ignored in discussions of quality improvement.

In response to these remarks, a committee member indicated that HCFA does have a Medicare risk measure. It is known as the Health Outcomes Study, which was designed to compare plan performance in the care of the Medicare risk enrollees. However, this study relies on random selection of patients from each plan's membership rather than selection of patients based on data. Plans are blinded to the selection process. Results from the study provide a quality audit rather than a measure of the effectiveness of different treatment interventions among plans.

HEALTH CARE POLICY AND INSURANCE IMPLICATIONS OF DEFINING SERIOUS OR COMPLEX MEDICAL CONDITIONS

A panel of three speakers addressed issues associated with health care policy and the insurance implications of defining serious or complex medical conditions. The three panel members were Dr. Helen L. Smits, Dr. Lynn M. Etheredge, and Mr. Stan Jones. The session opened with remarks from Dr. Smits concerning issues related to the range of managed care plans, the response of plans' medical directors to the issue of serious or complex conditions, and potential risks and concerns associated with plans of care.

Managed Care and Approaches to Regulation

Dr. Smits noted that people writing and talking about managed care today still tend to think about the original Kaiser staff model. This was essentially an arrangement in which the insurance plan was buried in a provider system that owned ambulatory care, specialty care in the original Kaiser model, and the actual hospital beds and other facilities. This is one extreme model of managed care. In contrast, one can consider the Oxford system. In this, an insurance company contracted with providers in a fairly wide range of ways to provide services. These are the two extremes of managed care, and regulations concerning serious or complex medical conditions must encompass both models.

In fact, the managed care industry also involves many big indemnity plans or network-type managed care plans. These types of plans enter into risk-sharing arrangements with providers, which is somewhat similar to the original Kaiser model of care. Under such a model, the physician may have within his or her care team a fair amount of control over what resources are going to be available to specific patients. Dr. Smits then addressed issues related to case management in different types of managed care plans. Most medical directors of plans would begin to identify categories of patients with serious or complex medical conditions by collecting information from their case managers about the types of patients they are managing.

Case management would be very tightly related to the process of patient care within a Kaiser-type model of managed care, a staff model health maintenance organization, or a physician group accepting risk. There would be a provider giving care within the constraints of a care planning process. Someone may be named as case manager, usually a nurse or a social worker. The plan of care would usually be developed in full collaboration with, and with the knowledge of, the patient. It is likely that the patient would know the identity of the case manager. The patient would also have some involvement in the creation of the plan of care, although the degree of involvement would depend on the attitudes and preferences of the health care team. This health care team would be similar to the team described by Dr. Lynn to provide specialty care.

The classic network-type plan would also rely on case managers, often either social workers or nurses. These case managers would be very sophisticated and well trained. In many instances they would have very sophisticated computer support to inform them about the patient. However, they usually would not know the patient personally and would not interact with the patient other than by telephone. Their work would be primarily with providers. They would manage cases and try to put together a package of services, which would be authorized and paid for, that suited the needs of a patient with a complex medical condition, such as a pregnant methadone addict with severe congestive heart failure. Such a patient would need services in the home as well as require more than one kind of medical care. The case manager in the plan would generally know who is providing care to this patient and who is authorizing the services. It is likely that a case manager for a patient with a serious and complex condition would be unknown to the member, and the care planning process also would be unknown to the member.

Under this model of managed care, providers with contracts for services would be responsible for developing the plans of care. Network health plans might, in the process of making case management decisions about complex cases, receive copies of a care plan, or discuss it over the phone with the provider, or record elements of it in the computer. However, the case manager would not be responsible for developing the plan of care. Rather, the professionals involved in providing care to the patient would develop the care plan.

Dr. Smits provided the network model of case management and plans of care in order to suggest to the committee that the development of a care plan increases the likelihood of duplicating or replicating in some way an activity that really belongs in the provider's hand. This has its own potential for creating complexities in the caregiving process. She stressed that many managed care plans are very different from the traditional Kaiser model with respect to case management and the development of care plans.

Dr. Smits then reflected on some of the details of plans of care. She reiterated that there is a wide range of people with serious and complex conditions. On the one hand, there are the elderly, particularly the old old and the dying elderly. On the other hand, there are considerably younger people, often with one primary illness such as HIV/AIDS that is associated with a series of problems. A plan of care is, almost by definition, something that is wanted by providers. However, it is essential to ensure that plans of care do not become a coercive activity. The core of the Consumers' Bill of Rights is to protect consumers, at least in one way, by making sure that they have access to specialists of their choice.

For example, a patient has been going to the same neurologist for 5 years for a condition that is progressively deteriorating. This provider is associated with Hospital A. The patient also knows that friends with the same chronic condition go to Hospital B in order to see another neurologist in the same network but with a different approach to treatment. According to the patient's plan of care, she or he has had sufficient access to a neurologist and all necessary tests. However, the patient wants to see the neurologist at Hospital B in order to have access to the alternative treatment. The patient wants the right to see the second neurologist.

Dr. Smits reminded the committee of the importance of not developing regulations that support efforts by plans to exert excessive control over issues that are properly individual decisions about care. People ought to have the right to make choices about their care and care providers. Medicare beneficiaries, especially the disabled, should have the right to make up their own minds when they want to walk out of one plan of care and into another. It is equally important to ensure that the regulations do not advocate for an audit process that identifies managed care systems as lacking treatment or care plans in instances when patients have chosen not to follow the suggested plan of care.

Dr. Smits went on to note that fully 50 percent of all of the individuals who now participate in clinical trials at the National Institutes of Health (NIH) are self-referred. Many locate information about these trials directly through Internet sites, by contacting the 800 numbers established for the trials, or by calling the NIH directly to request information about possible trials. Such self-referrals are a radical change over the last 5 years, and many of the people self-referring to these trials are likely to have a serious or complex medical condition such as cancer. These patients have chosen to walk away from the providers who were involved with their original diagnosis and treatment plan. In many instances, they will self-refer to a clinical trial while not informing the members of their original care team. This pattern of self-referral will be important to consider in any definition or treatment plan for serious and complex medical conditions. It has implications both for the committee's definition of serious or complex conditions and for any regulations that emerge from this definition.

Dr. Smits also urged the committee to consider recommendation of regulations that would facilitate access to certain special privileges within a health plan by patients who are defined as having serious and complex conditions. An example of such a special service might be to provide patient access to the plan of care. Currently, network-type health plans have no obligation to reveal the care plan to the member. Patient access to the care plan would be most important in instances of disputes about care. Similarly, Dr. Smits cited the issue of advance appeal mechanisms as a potential special service for patients with serious or complex conditions. There may be instances where a case manager will have a plan of care outlining treatment for the upcoming nine months. The patient, however, disagrees with this plan. Under such circumstances, appeals should not be delayed until an x-ray or physical therapy does not occur as soon as the patient expects. In fact, Dr. Smits advocated that the patient be able to appeal the plan as it is laid out for however long in the future.

The issue of continuity of care was also emphasized in Dr. Smits's remarks. In fact, discontinuity in care coordination occurs with disturbing frequency in the current health care delivery system. For example, a plan writes a contract with someone to provide pharmacy or mental health services; the next day these providers have been sold to someone else or somebody else has replaced the provider group. A health plan may have a contract with a large doctor group. Suddenly, a second plan offers them a special deal if they become exclusive providers. Consequently, a sizable proportion of members in the first plan choose to go with the second plan in order to continue with their provider or simply change plans because they did not like their choice of providers in the first plan. This is a time of very rapid change in the delivery and reimbursement of health care services. It is essential that consumers receive protections to ensure that they can make their own health care choices. Conversely, protections are necessary for consumers in order to ensure continuity of care when contracts change or expire.

In summarizing her thoughts, Dr. Smits urged the committee to consider carefully the issues of chronicity, persistence, and progressive deterioration in the definition of serious or complex medical conditions. She specifically cited pregnancies covered by Medicaid plans, which can involve serious and complex conditions that are ultimately resolved when the pregnancy ends. This does not mean that the conditions are any less serious or complex or that the patient is any less entitled to special protections during pregnancy. Other examples of serious or complex conditions that eventually resolve include some cancers, severe infections, and episodic crises for patients with HIV/AIDS. These conditions are more prevalent in younger populations. It is important not to label a patient as serious or complex for a lifetime, particularly when payment systems are not adaptable if, in fact, the medical condition changes over time.

The committee requested clarification and additional details from Dr. Smits on a number of issues. Specifically, she was asked about members of the HealthRight, Inc., managed care plan with serious or complex medical conditions and whether their classification as serious or complex had any relationship to the amount of money being spent on them? Dr. Smits agreed that enrollees with serious or complex health conditions were likely to appear on a printout of the highest-expenditure patients over a period of 5 or 6 months. It was suggested that expenditure of resources might be one method of identifying patients with serious or complex medical conditions. Dr. Smits was then asked if patients with serious or complex medical conditions would comprise the top 1 percent of the highest-expenditure patients.

In response, Dr. Smits pointed out that the most expensive members in Medicaid managed care are premature babies. The costs are overwhelming during the time these infants are hospitalized. A plan of care was established for the interval of hospitalization, but after discharge there is not a great deal of care management for these infants. She pointed out that if a health care plan looked just at the most costly 1 percent of its enrollees, many premature infants would be identified, but the plan would miss people with serious or complex conditions who comprise the top 5 or 10 percent of total expenditures.

Dr. Smits was also asked if a premature infant would still be considered a serious or complex patient after discharge from the hospital. She acknowledged that this was likely to be the case immediately following discharge because the infant would most likely require some home care. Case management would continue for those infants with serious disabilities. In contrast, some infants would be released to home quite healthy, and after 4 or 6 months, if the mother is reliable about follow-up visits, further case management would not be required.

Dr. Smits was also queried about when a managed health care plan would decide that case management was no longer necessary for a specific patient. She acknowledged that the final answer to this is not yet known but suggested that it might be when requests for services are discontinued. She also noted that in some cases, there would be a very clear cutoff point. For example, a severely ill pregnant woman would require intensive case management including home services until the birth of the baby. Following the birth, special services continue on a tapered basis for the first 3 months and then are usually no longer required. Dr. Smits advocated for managed care plans using good computer systems for case management that will allow the case manager to close a case but also generate a reminder in 4 or 6 months to follow-up with the patient or provider to determine current health status and needs.

A similar question about duration and scope of case management for disabled children was raised. Dr. Smits explained that such children would require one or more case managers or care coordinators because of their eligibility from birth to 3 years of age for services that may well include non-Medicaid services, so as to ensure access to early invention programs and Title V services. She pointed out that although Medicaid would not be the payment source for such ancillary services, the Medicaid case manager would be expected to know where these services could be found. There would be an incentive to find them and link the member to them at every level, from low-level services such as locating certain kinds of equipment or furniture for use in the home to very high-level services such as access to specialized training and education programs. Establishing links to community services would be an essential aspect of the Medicaid case manager's responsibilities.

APPENDIX A

The committee explored in further detail Dr. Smits's remarks concerning special protections. She was asked to define what these special protections might be and what they might protect against. In response, Dr. Smits referred to the proposed final regulations from HCFA for the Medicare+Choice program. According to Dr. Smits's interpretations of the original legislative language for the Consumers' Bill of Rights, people with serious and complex conditions may not be receiving as good care as they should be from managed care. Some of these patients are doing fine and do not require any protections. Having the right to know about things such as their plan of care, the right to appeal forward, and similar rights will help people who are dissatisfied with the services provided by their managed care plan to improve their situation. Special protections may be necessary if patients are to have at their disposal all of the possible tools to obtain good care on their own behalf. Dr. Smits cautioned the committee that her remarks about special protections were not intended to imply that everybody is dissatisfied with the care provided by their health plan. Rather, the term was used in a generic sense to address consumer protections in health care.

Dr. Smits was further queried about the issue of special protections and whether they should protect patients from certain events or rather ensure access to special services. She clarified that special protections would apply to ensure that patients received the care they chose instead of the care that their doctor(s) wanted to provide. The committee commented that remarks from earlier presentations by Dr. Lynn and Ms. Brody advocated strongly for case management for patients with serious or complex conditions, in which one individual assumes responsibility for coordinating all aspects of the requisite care. Dr. Smits generally concurred with this perspective but suggested that it might not apply as well for the elderly or for patients who do not want details about certain aspects of their health (e.g., mental health treatments) revealed to their primary care provider. Efforts to maintain the privacy and confidentiality of patients can often result in giving them control over what information is to be shared.

Pursuing this line of thought, Dr. Smits was asked if providers would need to be exempt from liability for full responsibility for patient care in instances where they were uninformed about aspects of a patient's medical care and health status. In responding, Dr. Smits used Connecticut as an example. Under current Connecticut law, the provider cannot know about mental health services or family-planning services unless specific permission has been given by the patient for such information to be released by the health care plan. Similarly, in New York State, health plans cannot provide primary care providers with lists of all medications taken by their patients. To do so could result in disclosure of information about patient use of psychopharmaceutical agents because in doing so, the plan would reveal information about mental health care services. Dr. Smits acknowledged that this presents significant challenges to primary care providers who must be absolved from responsibility for mistakes that could be attributed to lack or inadequacy of information. However, privacy is a very significant issue for most patients.

The committee then turned its attention to Dr. Smits's remarks about providing members of managed care plans with an advance appeal mechanism for specific aspects of the care plan. It was pointed out that Medicare currently has an extensive external appeals mechanism in place that permits patients to appeal any denial of a service of any sort. Dr. Smits was asked if she was suggesting that the existing Medicare mechanism should be expanded to give beneficiaries the right to appeal a care plan for external review. Dr. Smits elaborated further on her comments first by pointing out that a denial of service means that a claim has been submitted and not paid or a request has been made to authorize a service and the request has been denied. For example, a physician wants to do magnetic resonance imaging (MRI) on a patient. The plan is contacted by the provider for approval of this test, which is denied. The provider can appeal this decision under the current Medicare appeals process. Dr. Smits suggested that people with serious and complex medical conditions should be allowed to review their plan of care and to proactively appeal elements of the plan with which they disagree. These patients should have opportunities to appeal future events outlined in care plans in order to eliminate the delays that occur under the current system of denial.

Dr. Tony Hausner of HCFA provided further clarification of some of Dr. Smits's remarks. First he noted that the regulations for Medicare+Choice require that a care or treatment plan be developed for all persons with serious or complex conditions. In response to questions from plans about giving beneficiaries the right to approve these care plans, HCFA encouraged managed care organizations to allow the beneficiary to participate in the development of the treatment plan but did not mandate it. Dr. Hausner also noted that the proposed final regulations for Medicare+Choice have requirements for coordination of care, especially for persons with serious or complex conditions. These requirements are contained in Section 422.112, Access to Services, of the *Federal Register* publication of the final rules concerning establishment of the Medicare+Choice program (*Federal Register,* June 26, 1998).

With respect to Dr. Smits's comments about appeals, Dr. Hausner clarified that the plan of care can be appealed to an external organization. He suggested that a grievance process would apply in such instances where a patient would want to express disagreement with his or her plan of care. He also expressed strong support for case management systems and recommended Sierra Health Services in Nevada as a very comprehensive case management system that would merit consideration by the committee.

Dr. Smits suggested that HCFA consider reimbursement of providers for the time taken to prepare plans of care. Payment for a mandated service such as the development of care plans would seem to be appropriate. The committee acknowledged the importance of Dr. Smits's observations about issues of personal control over health care decisions and the complexities posed by the expression of such personal controls. It was pointed out that Medicare still provides enrollees with choices about whether to be in a managed care or a fee-for-service indemnity plan. Dr. Smits was asked if she believed that persons enrolled in managed care plans should have the same amount of free choice as persons enrolled in indemnity plans. Do you tell patients enrolled in managed care plans who request more choices and involvement in their care plan to switch to a fee-for-service plan? Alternatively, do you explain to the patient that certain guidelines and management rules are associated with the choice to enroll in a managed care plan? Dr. Smits pointed out that health care reform is moving toward a time when patient choice will no longer be as easy or frequent as it is even now. However, if patients are locked in for a year to a specific Medicare managed care organization, they need some protection of their right to make choices about their health care. Dr. Smits expressed doubt that Medicare members who have chosen managed care should be entitled to absolute, total free choice. She concluded that for the elderly enrolled in Medicare managed care plans, privacy and confidentiality will be equally as important as the right to independence and personal choice.

Implementation Strategies for the Medicare+Choice Regulations Concerning Serious or Complex Medical Care

The remarks of Dr. Lynn M. Etheredge addressed possible implementation strategies for the Medicare+Choice regulations concerning patients with complex or serious medical conditions. He focused particularly on some policy context for thinking about data systems in Medicare and actually making such systems work to produce change. Dr. Etheredge acknowledged that Medicare has had much more experience in developing regulatory requirements in data systems than in actually using data systems effectively to bring about changes in health care delivery. Issues addressed by data systems include fundamental questions of taxonomy—what is medical care and how it should it be organized? Often the data systems involve multiple agendas and multiple organizational responsibilities. Medicare plans try to determine who is reporting to whom for what purpose and to identify appropriate uses for data. In doing so, one is actually trying to define a health care system in a health care environment in which such systems do not occur naturally or, if they do, are organized around medical disciplines and individual institutional roles.

Dr. Etheredge suggested that these issues reflect a very early stage of managed care. Efforts are ongoing to answer questions about the type and extent of management that should be provided by managed care plans, especially for patients with serious or complex medical conditions. If not case management for serious or complex conditions, what is managed care doing in addition to limiting costs? The issue of defining serious or complex medical conditions raises some fundamental issues of accountability: who is accountable, how are they held accountable, and what is the heart of managed care? Such discussions begin by examination of current ways of thinking, conceptualizing, and defining medical activity. However, the earlier remarks by Mr. Crowley, and Drs. Durant and Lynn, emphasized that current concepts of care delivery and management do not relate very well to issues that arise for plans providing care to patients with serious, chronic, and complex medical problems.

Currently, managed care is organized either around institutions such as hospitals or, more frequently, around the practice of fee-for-service medicine. Data are readily available to count numbers of physician visits, medical and laboratory tests, admissions to hospitals, and visits to emergency rooms. In contrast, data to describe improvements in patient health status, effectiveness of treatments for diabetes or cancer, or failures to improve health status are not readily available or reported.

Dr. Etheredge cited the recent report of the Institute of Medicine National Cancer Policy Board on quality of care for cancer patients. The report demonstrated that answers to questions about the quality of care received by cancer patients are not readily available. Existing data systems to monitor and measure quality of care are only in the very early stages of development. The report included a number of ambitious recommendations to respond to this informational gap. Specifically, measures to assess quality of care have to be developed. Benchmarks for standards of quality care for cancer patients should be established.

Dr. Etheredge urged the committee to consider the recommendations of the National Cancer Policy Board report and identify those areas that would be representative of the issues relevant to serious or complex medical conditions. He also recommended that the committee view its policy challenge as one of initiating a process of developing a quality management and reporting system for patients with serious or complex medical conditions that would apply to both managed care and fee-for-service plans. He argued that the two types of plans should apply similar, if not the same, standards of care for patients with serious or complex medical conditions. Dr. Etheredge advocated for an outcome or set of outcomes that would be both useful and future oriented.

Medicare has tens of thousands of pages of regulations, and it is very easy to take any problem that occurs and write more regulations about it. The problem is actually getting anyone to apply these regulations to the practice of health care. Dr. Etheredge emphasized that any requirements or regulations resulting from the committee's deliberations on serious or complex medical conditions should be something people can apply and find useful today. Such regulations should also include support for efforts to build a new kind of quality system, measurement system, or accountability system for the future, in recognition of the fact that there will be several more evolutions beyond what this committee is able to accomplish within a limited time.

Dr. Etheredge made reference to some of Medicare's previous experiences with trying to change the medical care system and get it to behave in different ways by defining and classifying certain kinds of patients and constructing payment systems around these new classifications. For example, the development of diagnosis-related groups (DRGs) was probably the most ambitious attempt to reform the Medicare classification system. It took more than 10 years to accomplish and was developed by quality assurance engineering experts at Yale. The DRG system tried to move beyond per day and per admission to define a diagnosis and a procedure to which modern management techniques could be applied. This would allow Medicare to manage the system, measure the quality, measure the cost, pay on this basis, and complete the health system on this basis. The DRG system came from a whole different paradigm that attempted to define patients in terms of needs and then follow through with specific procedures to fulfill these needs. The greatest impact of the DRG classification has probably been on payment systems, although there may be some cases in which providers are managing quality on this basis.

Examples of other areas with experience relevant to the efforts of the committee to define serious or complex medical conditions might include the following:

1. coverage of kidney disease patients and other serious or complex conditions, combined with efforts to build payment systems and quality assurance around these categories of patients;
2. hospice care;
3. nursing home care and regulations, especially those focused on issues of quality assurance, plans of care, and related requirements;
4. efforts by HCFA to define Centers of Excellence for interventions such as coronary artery bypass surgery and to establish benchmarks for state-of-the-art plans and providers; and finally,
5. risk adjustment using adjusters that are better predictors of health care utilization than patient age, gender, welfare status, nursing home status, and so forth.

Dr. Etheredge noted that many of the better predictors of health care utilization might include race, socioeconomic status, and patient status as alive or dead. He commented that these are not necessarily socially or politically correct, and many of them would be susceptible to gaming if they were used. Problems arise, however, when efforts are made to label or categorize people. He concluded that the most effective methods for patient categorization would combine clinical and actuarial data. In order to impact the health care delivery system, plans will have to pay for better care or give people choices to select their own care. In the absence of a payment system that is integrated with data systems on quality, there will be a tendency to have the regulators fighting against economic incentives, and economic incentives usually will win.

Dr. Etheredge also noted that in general, managed care organizations have focused on populations under age 65. This is where most of their expertise has been obtained. People who are terminally ill and all of the Medicare beneficiaries who are going to die due to the processes of aging are very different kinds of populations. Many of the things that managed care plans do or have done for people under 65—for example, triaging people away from specialists and primary care—will frequently have to be reversed to meet the needs of elderly populations. It is important to note that current and new managed care plans will not have the expertise to meet the needs of the elderly Medicare populations.

Despite this lack of expertise, there is a real need to provide beneficiaries with assurances that plans of care will be developed and followed and that care management is in place and intended to improve the lives of patients rather than conceal efforts to ration care.

Case managers will be among the first users of definitions of patient categories such as serious or complex. If these definitions are well conceptualized, they can accomplish a number of goals. They can identify patients who actually need more services. They can get patients to agree that they need more services. They can help case managers to coordinate care and can even allow clinicians who choose to specialize to compete for patients on the basis of the specialty care they can provide. It would be very useful to have competition on this basis, but in order to do so, systems are going to be required that not only define patients but also offer choices and resources to provide care. This is one reason that actuaries will have to become involved in some of this work.

In Dr. Etheredge's opinion, the health care system is moving in the direction of providing patients with more choices than are currently available. Patients diagnosed with a particular illness such as cancer, congestive heart failure, chronic obstructive pulmonary disease, or stroke will be offered a series of choices that would allow them to enter specialized care programs having a partial capitation payment. This would allow the development and organization of care delivery systems that would compete to take care of stroke patients or patients with any of these other conditions. To accomplish this, it would be necessary to have criteria to define clinically relevant populations at need, as well as actuarial data about these populations that would support the calculation of some costs for care, to ensure that there really is effective choice and incentive for competition.

This type of information would also be useful to health plan managers, especially network managed care plans, in which contracts must be established with health care providers to ensure access and delivery of services to patient populations. Such plans then have a choice of different providers of care in different settings. If plans were able to define patients with needs for particular arrays of service, they could then begin to monitor the effectiveness of these treatment services and develop strategies for more equitable cost management. This information would support the efforts of health plan managers to do a better job of managing and selecting their own providers. In turn, the boards of health care plans would have information to hold their own managers accountable and compare the performance of cost plans to see how well they are doing.

External reviewers should be available to meet audit requirements imposed by the Joint Commission on Accreditation of Hospitals, National Commission on Quality Assurance, and state regulators. It is essential to be able to examine a plan and determine if the quality of care represents the state of the art or standards for acceptable quality.

Finally, Dr. Etheredge argued that purchasers need a well-designed data system for chronically ill patients to begin to determine if they are getting value for the money. In most populations, including Medicare, about 5 percent of the population uses 50 percent of the care and 20 percent of the population uses about 80 percent. This allows health care plans to focus on a fairly small number of patients and have good control over the expenditure of resources.

Dr. Etheredge also encouraged the committee to consider patients who are dual eligible for both Medicare and Medicaid. This includes about 6 million people who use about 30 to 35 percent of the resources from both programs. These are expensive, complex, and difficult patients, and HCFA and states are trying to develop new systems that would support reporting on the quality of care provided for these patients.

Dr. Etheredge strongly urged the committee to consider a continuum of options, starting from the very simple option of saying there has to be a plan of care, involvement of a specialist, and a few things to be checked off and audited for patients with serious or complex medical conditions. This should then be expanded to include consideration of systems of care that can take care of both patients younger than 65 years with a need for acute care and an older population that is increasingly defined by chronic and multiple health problems requiring coordination of care by many providers. Such a system of care should involve the patient, family members, and professionals working together to determine patient needs and strategies to manage lives that are increasingly limited by disabling diseases.

He further suggested that the committee should decide what point to choose on that continuum of options. If the committee selects definitions and regulations that are more limited in nature with a greater likelihood of immediate usefulness, it will be equally important to set in motion a series of recommendations, perhaps similar to those of the National Cancer Policy Board. Such recommendations would better define who is accountable and how the system would work in response to more complex options. The initial efforts of the committee should form the foundation for building a better system of care management and better system of choice for all patients. The committee was encouraged to ensure that its recommendations, especially those associated with quality assurance improvement efforts, would be coordinated with similar efforts underway by Dr. Lynn and her colleagues and the National Commission on Quality Assurance.

In closing, Dr. Etheredge encouraged the committee to consider its efforts as part of an overall, ongoing strategy to build a better system to provide care to all patients, especially those with serious or complex medical conditions. The work of the committee should establish a foundation from which many other uses and users can develop.

The committee requested that Dr. Etheredge expand on his comments concerning application of the DRG system to the development of possible definitions for serious or complex medical conditions. In response, Dr. Etheredge described an ongoing, collaborative research effort in which he is trying to define new delivery systems for terminally ill patients. This effort requires the involvement of clinicians to review epidemiological data to identify the major causes of death. Actuaries then review Medicare data to determine what can be known about the actual experience of diagnosing and treating these conditions. There is particular interest in defining the number of patients with one or multiple conditions and assessing costs and variations in cost for care. Dr. Etheredge also referenced work done in collaboration with HCFA in which epidemiological and cost data for chronic obstructive pulmonary disease and congestive heart failure were reviewed. These analyses can yield estimates for capitation payments for patients with these two health conditions. He suggested that specific cancers would also be amenable to this approach, and he referred to stand-alone cancer care centers that are competing for the business of managed care plans.

The committee pointed out that by and large managed care in this country is discounted fee for service. Dr. Etheredge was asked to address the distinctions between things over which managed care plans have direct control and factors associated with the behaviors of health care providers who work for multiple, different plans including some fee-for-service and some managed care plans. It was pointed out that one of the main reasons the committee had been formed was to address the issue of inequitable access to specialty care. More specifically, the committee had been asked to determine if there are some benefits ensuring access to specialty care that are available to people with fee-for-service plans and not available to those receiving health care coverage from managed care plans. From this perspective, a second question was raised by the committee about whether managed care plans are being asked to develop a "miracle" health care delivery system to deal with the needs of persons with serious or complex medical conditions.

Dr. Etheredge agreed that the managed care industry is likely to be worried about whether it will suddenly be required to solve every problem in the health care system. In response to the question about whether it is appropriate to view providers and health care plans as separate or integrated entities, Dr. Etheredge opined that the two are an entity if the plan is a managed care plan. The integration of the two is part of what is sold about managed care companies, and consequently, managed care plans should be held legally responsible for the care that is being delivered. If the managers of the managed care company do not know who has a serious or complex conditions and are not monitoring the quality of care being provided to these patients, who is and for what are they being paid? Dr. Etheredge further elaborated that there is a reason to treat managed care companies as an entity because they put themselves forward as an entity to manage care. He suggested that it will be important to use similar approaches to reform fee-for-service plans and develop a continuum of options, particularly for the chronically ill and terminally ill, that would pay for programs of care on a mixed capitation–fee-for-service basis.

Dr. Etheredge noted that part of the problems with managed care is the current payment system. If a plan is losing money or struggling to survive in a competitive environment, most directors of managed care plans will look first at their enrollees who are costing them $20,000, $30,000, or $60,000 a year. This may result in a reduction in provision of the services of specialists. Such problems might be resolved if Medicare moves away from pure capitation toward mixed capitation and fee for service as a basic way of paying for health plans. Alternative payments plans will be of particular importance for high-cost patients. Identifying the types of patients who would benefit most from these new kinds of payment systems will be a useful and important first step.

Dr. Etheredge was also asked his opinion of the feasibility of developing payment systems for illnesses that have reasonably defined futures that could lead to the determination of a lifetime charge for the management of these illnesses, no matter the final outcome. Dr. Etheredge concurred with this approach. He pointed out that it raises a very fundamental issue about the nature of disease in medical care—that is, how much of it is predictable and manageable for what populations? This approach also requires that outliers be eliminated from the payment equation. It remains to be determined how many of the serious and complex conditions can be considered predictable and manageable after the outliers are removed. Dr. Etheredge's research with Dr. Lynn suggests that lifetime costs can be determined for patients diagnosed with congestive heart failure and chronic obstructive pulmonary disease. Calculating these costs and managing these conditions well results in a significant amount of savings. In the absence of good disease management, patients ultimately seek care in emergency room visits that are quite costly. Systems such as those implemented by Kaiser for patients with congestive heart failure, which involve a daily telephone call to check on health status and weight, can be effective in preventing predictable crises and keeping patients out of emergency rooms. This, in turn, saves a lot of money.

There may be other conditions for which case management and cost savings are not possible due to the nature of the illness. It is extremely important however, to try to manage care over the long term for parts of the Medicare population rather than provide episodic care with discounted fee for service. To the extent that effective care management systems can be developed for specific patient populations, efforts should be devoted to building these systems. Other patient populations may have to continue with episodic care management. Dr. Etheredge suggested that the committee advocate for research programs to begin to resolve these issues so that managed care companies will actually be able to manage care in predictable ways for improving outcomes. At the moment, this is very difficult for almost anyone to do.

The committee also discussed with Dr. Etheredge the issue that disaggregated systems of health care payment further exacerbate problems caused by a poorly coordinated health care delivery system. It was noted that one recent policy change resulted in limiting home care visits to homebound patients, which could alter or have adverse effects on the costs and even the outcomes of certain chronic diseases. Many patients such as diabetics and those suffering congestive heart failure had received home services in the past although these patients were not necessarily homebound. They did, however, benefit from home visits to maintain their condition. Dr. Etheredge was asked his opinions about the possible impact of such a policy change regarding home health and how it might affect the whole continuum of care and the management of chronic disease.

In reply, Dr. Etheredge noted that there is great concern and suspicion about adding new entitlements such as home health or case management as an open-ended benefit. The cost implications of such open-ended benefits could be staggering. Dr. Etheredge cited a previous publication in which he and his colleagues suggested that case management should be targeted to specific patients who meet specific criteria. Such care could best be delivered through preferred provider organizations (PPO) type contracts. Case management organizations should be selected competitively, and the patient's physician and the patient should select them so that they are responsive to what they want and the kind of care that is developed in the care plan.

Dr. Etheredge also pointed out that the issue of fragmentation of payment systems is not particularly relevant to Medicare populations. There is Medigap coverage, but Medicare is so dominant and large today (and will continue to grow in the near future) that if Medicare pays for something for the elderly, other components of the health care delivery system start to provide these services as well. If Medicare doesn't pay for something, such as new programs for the chronically ill and so forth, other plans tend not to provide these services. So there is the opportunity to define a new system here using $200 billion a year of purchasing power. This is a nice resource to support efforts to reform the health system. If however this purchasing power is not applied, new programs for certain patient populations such as those with serious or complex medical conditions will not develop. Furthermore, systems to ensure improved quality of care will not emerge because the resources will not be there to pay for them.

Dr. Etheredge's remarks prompted several comments and questions from Dr. Hausner of HCFA. First, Dr. Hausner asked if Dr. Etheredge's research collaboration with Dr. Lynn would be compatible with HCFA's effort to establish the diagnostic cost group system, which is almost ready for the first stage of implementation and will be based on inpatient diagnosis. The intention is to expand the system to include all the data systems that would provide opportunities to look at multiple medical conditions, not just the primary condition.

Dr. Etheredge explained that his work with Dr. Lynn involved efforts to determine if the Medicare population could be divided into groups, including categories for the five leading causes of death: heart and lung failure, cancer, stroke, and dementia. The next step would be to determine if a reliable clinical indicator could be found that would identify patients as members of one of these five groups. The final step would be to determine a reliable payment system based on such clinical information. In one sense, Dr. Etheredge suggested that his work with Dr. Lynn is moving away from HCFA's efforts with the diagnostic cost group system. The latter system is getting more and more sophisticated and more and more complex. The collaborative work with Dr. Lynn is more simplified, which is necessary to develop estimates of payment for care of patients with these five conditions. It may be that greater differentiation beyond the five conditions does not improve the predictive value. Patients with one of these five conditions will typically have six or seven other diagnoses as well, but this information may not contribute in a meaningful way toward prediction of health care costs. From these perspectives, the work of Drs. Etheredge and Lynn is not compatible with HCFA's efforts to develop the diagnostic cost group system.

Dr. Hausner also concurred with Dr. Etheredge's earlier remarks about the importance of moving toward payment plans that involve mixed capitation and fee for service. In fact, the work of Joe Newhouse and others in this field indicates that trying to take a purer capitation and adjusting it to all these sophisticated measures does not achieve a more fair system of paying plans and paying for patient care that is possible with a mixed capitation, fee-for-service system.

Dr. Hausner also noted that HCFA is concerned with improving the fee-for-service system as much as the managed care system. Consequently, it is working with HEDIS and the consumer assessment system and developing quality improvement projects for fee for service. He expressed the opinion that managed care is in the forefront in terms of developing some management systems that will improve quality care for chronic conditions as well as care for all patients in general. The assessment systems that are being put into place and case management systems are innovating disease management. Both managed care and fee for services need dramatic efforts to improve the coordination of patient care, but managed care seems to have made a number of strides in specific areas, and it will be important to apply these lessons to the fee-for-service system.

Serious or Complex Medical Conditions: Insurance Issues

The final speaker at the workshop was Mr. Stan Jones. Mr. Jones opened his remarks by suggesting to the committee that it may not be possible at this time to respond to the questions posed by HCFA in the charge to the committee. He argued that simply developing a definition of serious or complex medical conditions, including recommendations about when access to specialists should be provided for Medicare+Choice enrollees, fails to address the fundamental problems and challenges of the current health care delivery system. Committing the resources necessary to develop sound definitions for serious or complex medical conditions could begin to resolve some of these basic problems.

A fundamental problem is to ensure that higher-quality, better-coordinated care is available for really sick people. He noted that a primary obstacle to resolving this problem is the current lack of knowledge about ways to pay a fair price for people who cost a lot either to health care plans or to providers. Consequently, important financial disincentives have been built into the care delivery system, and there is a lack of confidence about the quality and coordination of a complex array of services. Mr. Jones noted a second fundamental problem—beneficiaries do not really know how to choose among providers or plans based on quality. Consumers do not know how to evaluate the quality of the care they are receiving, especially those with serious or complex medical conditions.

Mr. Jones then suggested to the committee that it follow an ongoing process to develop a definition for serious or complex medical conditions. This process would acknowledge that all serious or complex conditions cannot be defined at once. Some conditions may be readily apparent as serious or complex. The definition of serious or complex illness might include consideration of specific health conditions combined with consideration of issues of functional status. The list would likely grow over time, and it is unlikely that all persons with a serious or chronic condition have been identified. Mr. Jones emphasized that efforts to identify conditions as serious or complex would be part of an ongoing process. He further suggested that a number of different players should be involved in the process of identifying serious or complex conditions. These would include clinicians, insurers, actuaries, and sophisticated consumers.

Mr. Jones pointed out that the process of the National Committee for Quality Assurance for the development of quality standards might be applicable. The group of individuals involved with identification of serious or complex medical conditions could contact the National Committee for Quality Assurance to request a hearing to support the development of a new set of standards to select serious or complex conditions. The group should elicit external input and advice in determining if an area ought to be defined as serious or complex. It would also be important that the group have the capacity to advocate for more inclusive definitions of serious or complex medical conditions. This would help prevent different disease advocacy groups from advancing definitions that are more detailed and fragmented.

Mr. Jones emphasized that his suggested approach to defining serious or complex medical conditions must be conducted on an ongoing basis and that the committee should initiate the process. The committee should also try to identify some of the criteria that conditions must meet to be added to the list of serious or complex conditions. These criteria are likely to be added and refined over time.

In justifying his suggested approach, Mr. Jones pointed out that in the current system there are strong financial incentives not to invest capital and effort to improve the quality of care for high-cost populations. The premium level that insurers or providers receive for patients with serious or complex conditions is well below the costs they incur. As a consequence of these high-cost subscribers, the premium that the plan must charge for all of its subscribers must be increased, making the plan less competitive. Consequently, there is an incentive for plans and providers not to attract a lot of patients with serious or complex conditions that will incur high cost.

A fair payment plan for high-cost patients with serious or complex conditions is necessary to create incentives for both providers and plans to compete and enroll these people. A system of fair payment is likely to encourage plans and providers to invest capital and resources in improving the quality of care for this patient population. The development of fair payments will rely on data that allow HCFA, health care plans, and providers to develop accurate estimates of costs to care for these conditions. In fact, Mr. Jones argued that the availability of cost data should be one of the key criteria in determining what conditions are considered serious or complex.

Mr. Jones also noted that the distinction between one serious or complex illness and another—or between an ordinary, everyday garden-variety condition and a serious and complex condition—has to be clinically precise. In the absence of such clinical distinctions, providers will group diagnoses and try to bill for the best price possible. Providers must develop thoughtful and realistic prices for the care that is delivered. Unfortunately, at this time, providers are not usually very accurate or skilled in determining realistic estimates for cost of care. There are, however, organizations in this country that can work with providers to develop such estimates. Clear clinical definitions for serious or complex conditions, combined with the ability to accurately estimate costs of care for these conditions, will allow providers such as specialists to develop proposals for insurance companies to care for such patients. This can allow specialists the opportunity to get involved with health insurance and compete with other health care plans to provide an array of services for specific groups of patients.

Mr. Jones offered another reason for adhering to an ongoing process to identify serious or complex medical conditions. He suggested this as a method to hold HCFA more accountable for issues of quality of care. He observed that managed care plans have a deep suspicion that under traditional Medicare, people are not getting the quality of care that is available through other types of health plans. The ability to systematically define serious or complex conditions would allow tracking and comparisons of quality of care between Medicare and other reimbursement systems external to HCFA. This evaluation would be a method of discipline for traditional Medicare.

Yet another reason to engage in a systematic, ongoing process to define serious or complex medical conditions is to help beneficiaries understand better the services available to them and the quality of these services. Mr. Jones suggested that most consumers have difficulty in determining where they can get the best-quality care. This can be especially true for those with serious or complex medical conditions that require a full array of medical, social, emotional, and functional care services. Mr. Jones referenced his work with elderly patients. Providers can itemize a list of conditions and health problems confronting these patients. However, asking the patients to identify the problems often results in a different and much simpler list. This simpler list of health concerns forms the basis for their selection of a health care plan.

Mr. Jones then suggested that the committee consider a distinction between consumer choice at the point of service versus choice at the point of diagnosis. He asserted that patients get much more concerned and serious about providers and different types of health care plans when they are diagnosed with a condition. At this time, patients have a much greater understanding of the different types of care and service needs and wants. It may be at the point of diagnosis of a serious or complex medical condition that people under Medicare should have a choice among certified plans or the traditional Medicare program. The choice of health care plan may best be made at the time a patient is diagnosed with a serious or complex medical condition and advised about the types of services and care that will be required. Furthermore, Mr. Jones pointed out that if a reasonable reimbursement has been determined for the condition, it is likely that information and advertisements may be available to help patients decide which plans would best suit their needs. Such information might be provided by local specialty groups that have contracted with HCFA to provide services to patients with specific conditions for predetermined, equitable reimbursements. In larger metropolitan areas, patients might have several different specialty groups providing such information to them and making an effort to attract them. Mr. Jones concluded that this would be much more desirable than requiring plans or providers to let patients select specialists and go to them whenever they choose.

A committee member asked Mr. Jones for his opinions on different types of reimbursement mechanisms for special-needs patient groups. Specifically, he was asked to comment on the use of actuarially defined payments combined with stop-loss options as well as partial fee for service. In response, Mr. Jones suggested that the most realistic way to determine the appropriate amount of payment for patients with serious or complex medical conditions would be to solicit proposals for specific conditions. From HCFA's perspective, it would work best to identify a group of patients for whom services are required and realistic costs of care can be estimated. The Health Care Financing Administration could then request proposals from plans to provide care to these patient groups for the estimated capitation rates. Mr. Jones discouraged the use of a stop-loss approach to correct actuarially defined payments.

The committee also inquired about Mr. Jones's thoughts concerning plans' reactions to being held accountable with report cards. It was pointed out that report card information could be very useful for consumers and would allow them to "vote with their feet." Mr. Jones indicated that a report card that could evaluate the care and outcomes of a specific group of people with a similar category of serious or complex illness would be extremely informative to consumers. It is extremely important to provide consumers with information that is pertinent to their specific situation before they can do anything about it. The nearer you can get to a patient's specific situation, the more potent is the information going to be. He acknowledged, however, that such report cards have a number of limitations and that many plans will not have sufficient numbers of patients within a category to support meaningful analysis and interpretation of quality-of-care information. It would be important also to focus on institutional and other requirements that plans or HCFA might make in the interest of improving and monitoring quality of care.

Mr. Jones was also asked to comment on patient populations for whom cost estimation could not be developed because of lack of data. Potentially such patient groups might not be offered coverage and, as a result, might have the greatest need for a definition of serious or complex conditions and access to an array of services including care from specialists. Mr. Jones acknowledged the likelihood that there will be groups of patients who are difficult to categorize clinically and for whom a standardized reimbursement can be calculated. The whole issue of defining serious or complex medical conditions is quite large and unlikely to be solved completely for all patient groups. However, he urged the committee to begin the process of addressing issues related to defining serious or complex conditions and noted that information and data may become available in the future to address the needs of more difficult categories of patients.

Mr. Jones was asked to elaborate further on his conceptualization of consumer choice at point of diagnosis rather than point of service. Specifically, he was asked to identify some of the risks of such an approach and how these might be rationally apportioned in this context. In response, Mr. Jones expressed the opinion that a patient first becomes really interested in the delivery system when he or she is diagnosed with something that is complicated or serious and requires a lot of services. Insurance surveys indicate that prior to this point, consumers are likely to change plans and do not have a great deal of provider loyalty. They are motivated to find the best plan for the best deal, and they are not concerned about their provider because they do not see him or her very often. However, patients' interests and the need for choice change at the point of diagnosis. Mr. Jones asserted that at this point, the consumer becomes a patient who is serious and ready to look for the best options for his or her particular condition. These options might include the plan in which the patient is already enrolled, as well as some other choices of health care plans and providers. Information about these choices might be made available to a patient by the provider or by specific plans that are marketing specialized services to the patient. Ideally, this is when the person ought to choose, when plans should compete for patient loyalty, and when providers ought to compete for patient choice.

One committee member noted Victor Fuchs's assertion that there are two hierarchies of values—one that people employ when making purchasing decisions in health care, and one they employ when actually having to use the health care system. When consumers are well, their purchasing decisions are based largely on price. In contrast, consumers who become patients generally feel that price has no meaning when they need the services of the system. This raised the question of how risk could be spread actuarially in a way that would permit proactive management.

APPENDIX B

Speakers Biographies

KATHLEEN BRODY, P.H.N., is the project director for Model Care at Kaiser Permanente's Center for Health Research in Portland, Oregon. Since 1981, Ms. Brody has held several positions with Kaiser Permanente dealing primarily with health care research. Among them are project director for STORK, a program to prevent fetal and infant passive smoke exposure, organizational studies liaison, project data director, project administrator, and principal investigator. Ms. Brody has a B.S. in Nursing from California State University—Fresno and performed postbaccalaureate work in health care services and epidemiology. She has given numerous presentations on home care for the elderly, operational issues for the health maintenance (HMO) system, and HMO utilization for the last years of life. She is also widely published on issues related to health care for the elderly and frail.

JEFFREY S. CROWLEY, M.P.H., is deputy executive director for programs at the National Association for People with AIDS (NAPWA) in Washington, D.C. Previously, Mr. Crowley served as associate executive director and assistant executive director for NAPWA. In addition to his programmatic duties at NAPWA, Mr. Crowley conducts policy work on health care access issues, including Medicaid reform and managed care. He is cochair of the health task force of the Consortium for Citizens with Disabilities and a member of the National Academy of State Health Policy's Working Group on Medicaid Managed Care for People with AIDS. Mr. Crowley earned his B.A. in chemistry from Kalamazoo College in Michigan and an M.P.H. from Johns Hopkins University. He was formerly employed at the National Institutes of Health where he performed extensive research in biochemistry.

JOHN R. DURANT, M.D., is executive vice president of the American Society of Clinical Oncology, in Alexandria, Virginia. He is past vice president for health affairs and director of the Medical Center, University of Alabama at Birmingham, and past president of Fox Chase Cancer Center in Philadelphia. He has held various academic positions at the University of Alabama at Birmingham and Temple University. Dr, Durant is past president of the National Cancer Advisory Board and the Review Committee of the National Cancer Institute. He also served as president of the Association of American Cancer Institutes, the American Radium Society, and the American Society of Clinical Oncology. Dr. Durant earned his undergraduate degree at Swarthmore College and his M.D. at Temple University.

LYNN M. ETHEREDGE, Ph.D., is an independent consultant specializing in health-sector economics. He has helped to develop a number of health care reforms, including managed competition (as a principal of the Jackson Hole Group), a national quality improvement strategy, and the recent establishment of a National Health Care Purchasing Institute to advance quality-based purchasing by major public and private-sector payers. Previously, he was a senior executive with the federal government's Office of Management and Budget, where he headed its professional health staff and served during four administrations as its principal Medicare and Medicaid analyst. He is a founding member of the National Academy of Social Insurance and an author of more than 70 publications. Mr. Etheredge is a graduate of Swarthmore College.

STANLEY B. JONES, Ph.D., is a consultant to private foundations on competitive private health insurance markets and the roles of public policy in improving these markets. He was a founding partner of the Washington consulting firm, Health Policy Alternatives, Inc., and has served as vice president for Washington representation of the Blue Cross and Blue Shield Association and as a staff director of the Senate health subcommittee. Dr. Jones is chairman of the Advisory Committee to the Robert Wood Johnson Foundation State Initiatives in Health Care Financing Reform Program, a member of the U.S. Comptroller General's Health Advisory Committee, a trustee of the Alpha Center, and a member of the Institute of Medicine. His most recent work has focused on the policy, insurance, and health care issues associated with the chronically ill and frail elderly. He did his undergraduate work at Dartmouth College and graduate work at Yale University. He also serves as an Episcopal priest in the Diocese of West Virginia.

D. JOANNE LYNN, M.D., M.A., M.S., is the director of the Center to Improve Care of the Dying and professor of health care sciences and medicine at the George Washington University. She has held various academic positions including professor of medicine and community and family medicine at Dartmouth Medical Center. She has been an emergency room physician and triage physician at Washington Veterans Administration Hospital; an associate for medicine and humanities in the Division of Experimental Programs, George Washington University; a private practice locum tenens; an assistant director for medical studies on the President's Commission for the Study of Ethical Problems in Medicine and Biomedical Behavioral Research; medical director of the Washington Home; medical director of Hospice of Washington, and medical director of the George Washington Cancer Home Care Program. She participates in several professional societies including the Geriatric Society, the Hastings Center, the Institute of Medicine, the American Hospital Association, and the Veterans Health Administration. Dr. Lynn is widely published in topics related to hospice care and biomedical ethics. She earned her undergraduate degree at Dickinson College, her M.D. at Boston University, and her M.A. and M.S. at George Washington University and Dartmouth College, respectively.

HELEN L. SMITS, M.D., M.A.C.P., is president and chairman of HealthRight, Inc., in Meriden, Connecticut. Prior to joining HealthRight, Inc., she was deputy administrator for the Health Care Financing Administration; director of John Dempsey Hospital; professor of community medicine and health care at the University of Connecticut Health Center; and executive director of the John Dempsey Hospital Finance Corporation. Dr. Smits has served on many boards and committees of the Institute of Medicine, National Institutes of Health, Joint Commission on Accreditation of Health Care Organizations, Association of American Medical Colleges, and American College of Physicians. She earned her undergraduate degree from Swarthmore College, and her M.A. and M.D. at Yale University.

APPENDIX C

Workshop Agenda

WORKSHOP ON SERIOUS OR COMPLEX MEDICAL CONDITIONS

June 14, 1999
National Research Council
2001 Wisconsin Avenue, N.W.
Cecil and Ida Green Building, Room 130
Washington, D.C.

Closed Session
8:00–9:00 a.m.

Open Session
9:00 a.m.   Discussion with Sponsor
Tony Hausner, Project Officer, Health Care Financing Administration

9:45 a.m.   Break

10:00 a.m.   **SPEAKER PANEL**
Jeff Crowley, Executive Director, National Association of People with HIV/AIDS
"The Need for a Definition That Encompasses the Changing and Diverse Needs of People with Disabilities"

John Durant, Executive Vice President, American Society of Clinical Oncology
"The Complexities of Patients with Cancer"

Joanne Lynn, Director, Center to Improve Care of the Dying and Americans for Better Care of the Dying
"Serious-Complex as a Useful Category in Health Care Delivery"

Kathy Brody, Project Director for Model Care, Kaiser Permanente
"Population-Based Screening for Care Delivery Integration"

12:00 noon	Lunch
1:00 p.m.	**SPEAKER PANEL**

Helen Smits, President and Chair, HealthRight, Inc.
"Managed Care and Approaches to Regulation"

Lynn Etheredge, Consultant in Health Sector Economics
"Implementation Strategies for the Complex or Serious Conditions Requirement"

Stanley Jones, Consultant on Competitive Private Health Insurance Markets
"Serious and Complex Medical Conditions: Insurance Issues"

3:00 p.m.	Break
3:15 p.m.	Open Discussion
5:00 p.m.	Workshop Adjourn

APPENDIX D

Workshop Participants

Valerie Adelson, Assistant Director, Government Affairs, Epilepsy Foundation National Office, Landover, Maryland
Margaret Calvano, Senior Director, National Information Center on Epilepsy, Landover, Maryland
Robert Demichelist II, Brain Injury Association, Alexandria, Virginia
Albert Donnay, AIM, MCS Referral and Resources, Baltimore, Maryland
Murray Goldstein, Medical Director and Chief Operating Officer, UCP Research and Education Foundation, Washington, D.C.
Bob Greiss, Director, Center on Disability and Health, Washington, D.C.
Trisha Kurtz, Health Care Financing Administration, Washington, D.C.
Marian Scheinholtz, Practice Associate, American Occupational Therapy Association, Bethesda, Maryland
Rafael Semansky, Policy Research Analyst, Bazelon Center for Mental Health Law, Washington, D.C.
Sonia Tyutyulkova, Resident Psychiatrist, Sheppard Pratt Hospital, Baltimore, Maryland
Louise Zingeser, Director Health Care Services, American Speech-Language-Hearing Association, Rockville, Maryland

APPENDIX E

Committee Biographies

STEVEN S. SHARFSTEIN, M.D., M.P.A., is president, medical director, and chief executive officer for Sheppard Pratt Health System. Dr. Sharfstein has filled these positions since January 1992. He has also held the position of clinical professor and vice chair in the Department of Psychiatry at the University of Maryland since 1996. Previous positions held by Dr. Sharfstein include deputy medical director for the American Psychiatric Association from 1983 to 1986, associate director for behavioral medicine at the National Institute of Mental Health from 1980 to 1982, and director of the Division of Mental Health Service Programs at the National Institute of Mental Health from 1976 to 1980. Dr. Sharfstein also served as a member of the President's Advisory Commission on Consumer Protection and Quality in the Health Care Industry. Dr. Sharfstein received his B.A. from Dartmouth College, his M.P.A. from the John F. Kennedy School of Government in 1973, and his M.D. from the Albert Einstein College of Medicine in 1968. He holds membership in a number of professional societies including the American Psychiatric Association, Maryland Psychiatric Society, American College of Psychiatrists, American Medical Association, and American College of Mental Health Administration. He has served on the Institute of Medicine (IOM) Board on Neuroscience and Biobehavioral Health and the its Committee on Quality Assurance and Accreditation Guidelines for Managed Behavioral Health Care. Dr. Sharfstein has authored or edited a number of texts, and has published 150 professional articles and book chapters on a variety of clinical, economic, and administrative issues. He is currently editor of "Economic Grand Rounds," a quarterly column for the *Journal of Psychiatric Services*. He also serves on the editorial board for the *Journal of Mental Health Administration*.

WILLIAM E. GOLDEN, M.D., has been director of the Division of General Internal Medicine at the University of Arkansas for Medical Sciences, Little Rock, Arkansas, since 1984. In addition, he has been Associate Professor in the Department of Medicine at the University of Arkansas Medical School since 1990. Dr. Golden practices general internal medicine at the University of Arkansas and is board-certified in geriatrics. Dr. Golden received his B.A. from Brown University in Health Care Delivery in 1975 and his M.D. from Baylor College of Medicine, Houston, Texas, in 1978. Dr. Golden is a member of the Center for Outcomes Research and Evaluation, University of Arkansas Medical School and vice president for clinical quality improvement at the Arkansas Foundation for Medical Care. He has been a member of the University Hospital Managed Care Committee since 1996, and a member of the University Hospital Quality Cost-Effective Care Committee since 1998. Dr. Golden has continuing affiliations with the Accreditation Council for Continuing Medical Education, Agency for Health Care Policy and Research, American College of Physicians, American Health Quality Association, American Medical Association, Center for Clinical Quality Evaluation, and the American Society of Internal Medicine. Dr. Golden has also collaborated with the Health Care Financing Administration on the Work Group on the Evaluation of the PRO Program. In addition, Dr. Golden has served as a member of two IOM committees including the Committee on the Evaluation of the Uniform Clinical Assessment Program and Committee on Measuring the Health of Persian Gulf War Veterans. Dr. Golden has an extensive record of invited presentations to national professional groups and societies, as well as more than 50 publications in peer-reviewed journals.

SAM HO, M.D., is responsible for national quality improvement strategies at PacifiCare, including population health management, quality measurements and report cards, and continuous improvement of members' health outcomes. He is also active in national policy development and liaison with purchasers, providers, members, and industry colleagues. Prior to joining PacifiCare Health Systems, Dr. Ho successively served 3 years as vice president of Health Services, at PacifiCare of California and more than 10 years as senior executive and medical director at other major managed care organizations. He has also served as deputy director of health, medical director, and county health officer for the San Francisco Department of Public Health and has held academic faculty appointments at the schools of medicine and nursing at the University of California at San Francisco. Initially, his career included starting and maintaining a busy family practice in the most severe health manpower shortage area in San Francisco. The Honolulu native received his B.A. degree in sociology from Northwestern University, with Phi Beta Kappa honors, in 1972, and his medical degree from Tufts University School of Medicine in 1976. He completed his residency in family practice at the University of California at San Francisco, and has been a diplomate of the American Board of Family Practice since 1979. Dr. Ho currently is a member of several national advisory committees, representing physicians and managed care throughout the health care industry, and is actively involved in the debate on policy and direction in health care.

SHARON LEVINE, M.D., received her B.A. from Radcliffe College in 1967 and graduated with honors from Tufts University School of Medicine in 1971. Her clinical experience focused on pediatrics. She joined the Permanente Medical Group as staff pediatrician in 1977. Since 1991, Dr. Levine has been associate executive director of the Permanente Medical Group in Oakland, California. Dr. Levine has demonstrated expertise in a number of areas including human resource management, public relations, community and government relations, health policy, communication management, and diversity management. Her professional accomplishments include participation on a number of panels and boards such as the Association for Hospital Medical Education, Association of American Medical Colleges, National Association of Children's Hospitals, National Health Policy Forum, Society for Health Care Executives, and Alliance of Community Health Plans.

KATHLEEN H. McGINLEY, Ph.D., is assistant director of the ARC of the United States, Governmental Affairs Office. She received her B.A. in special education/mental retardation from Fontbonne College, St. Louis, Missouri, an M.A. in educational psychology and measurement from the University of Nebraska, Lincoln, and a Ph.D. in special education law and policy from the University of Kansas, Lawrence. Dr. McGinley has particular expertise in the areas of access to health care in both public and private health care delivery systems; consumer protections and quality measures to ensure that managed care meets the needs of individuals with mental retardation and other developmental disabilities; availability of housing options for people with disabilities; prevention of mental retardation and other developmental disabilities; and the effective implementation of programs authorized under the Developmental Disabilities Act. Dr. McGinley works closely with federal, state, and local government entities to identify, analyze, and guide policy development and implementation with the potential to benefit individuals with mental retardation and other developmental disabilities. Dr. McGinley has coordinated the legislative and grassroots efforts of both the Health and the Housing Task Forces of the Consortium for Citizens with Disabilities. She is editor and a major contributor to the ARC Government Report and legislative update for the Capitol Insider. Dr. McGinley staffs the ARC's Governmental Affairs Committee and is a liaison to the ARC's Health Promotion and Disability Prevention Committee. She is a member of the Patients' Bill of Rights Steering Committee.

GARTH SPLINTER, M.D., M.B.A., is an associate professor of family medicine at the University of Oklahoma College of Medicine and chief medical officer of University Hospital Trust. He is the former chief executive officer of the Oklahoma Health Care Authority (the Oklahoma Medicaid Agency). Dr. Splinter began his postsecondary education at the University of Oklahoma where he majored in industrial engineering. He received his B.S. degree in 1974. Dr. Splinter enrolled at Harvard University's business school where he earned his M.B.A. in 1976. He received his M.D. in 1984 from the University of Oklahoma. Following his family medicine residency, he joined the faculty at the University Health Sciences Center in 1987. During Governor David Walter's term, Dr. Splinter served as his special assistant on health care services. He has served as chair of the Commission on Oklahoma Health Care, medical director for the Employees Group Insurance Board, and principal investigator for the Robert Wood Johnson grant of State Initiatives on Health Care. Most recently, Dr. Splinter serves as the southwestern regional representative on the National Council of State Human Service Administrators (NCSHSA), and currently serves as health advisor to Governor Frank Keating.

NANCY A. WHITELAW, Ph.D., has been the associate director for the center for health system studies at Henry Ford Health System since 1993. In addition, Dr. Whitelaw serves as director of health services research for the Health Alliance Plan. Other appointments include research health science specialist for the Great Lakes Health Services, director for research and demonstration projects at the Department of Veterans Affairs, and staff investigator at the center for health systems studies at Henry Ford Health System. Dr. Whitelaw received her B.A. and M.S. in sociology from Portland State University and her Ph.D. in health services organization and policy from the University of Michigan in 1989. She has extensive research experience in minority aging, geriatric care, indicators of system performance, health care service utilization among veterans, and partnerships between major health systems and community health programs. Dr. Whitelaw's particular areas of expertise include managed care and the elderly, health status and health service utilization by elderly populations, use and organization of long-term care, and health status and health service use of urban populations. She has served on a number of national advisory boards and panels including work with the Health Care Financing Administration, National Institute on Aging, National Chronic Care Consortium, HMO Research Network, American Association of Health Plans, National Committee for Quality Assurance, and the Robert Wood Johnson Foundation. Dr. Whitelaw was a member of an IOM Committee to Develop an Agenda for Health Outcomes Research for Elderly People. She has a number of peer-reviewed journal articles and books as well as selected presentation and invited lectures. Dr. Whitelaw's professional affiliations include the Gerontological Society of America and the American Society on Aging.